£ 2.50

KU-515-307

Kitchen Suppers

Jenny Baker's interest in food began in her grandmother's kitchen in Devon, but it was only when she married that she seriously began to cook. She and her husband, James, lived for several years in the Middle East and later spent as much time as they could travelling to and discovering the food of other countries. In the seventies they ran a business in London catering for dinner parties and business functions. When their son and daughter left home for college, Jenny began to write about cooking. She divides her time between her two kitchens in London and France, and is now working on a collection of northern French recipes.

by the same author

THE STUDENT'S COOKBOOK

VEGETARIAN STUDENT

SIMPLY FISH

SIMPLE FRENCH CUISINE

Kitchen Suppers

JENNY BAKER

Illustrated by
JAMES BAKER

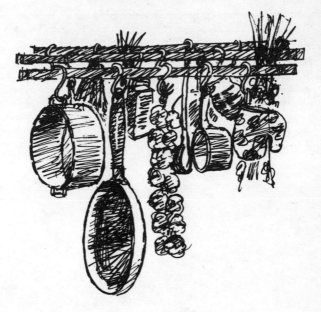

faber and faber
LONDON · BOSTON

First published in 1993 by
Faber and Faber Limited
3 Queen Square London WC1N 3AU

Phototypeset by Wilmaset Ltd, Wirral
Printed by Clays Ltd, St Ives plc

All rights reserved

© Jenny Baker, 1993
Illustrations © James Baker, 1993

Jenny Baker is hereby identified as author of this work
in accordance with section 77 of the Copyright, Designs
and Patents Act 1988.

*This book is sold subject to the condition that it shall not, by way of trade
or otherwise, be lent, resold, hired out or otherwise circulated without the
publisher's prior consent in any form of binding or cover other than that
in which it is published and without a similar condition including
this condition being imposed on the subsequent purchaser.*

A CIP record for this book
is available from the British Library
ISBN 0-571-16773-X

2 4 6 8 10 9 7 5 3 1

To my family and all those friends
with whom I've shared
kitchen suppers

Contents

Acknowledgements

Writing a cookery book is not a solitary pursuit – far from it. Everything must be tried and tested, and this is where family and friends come in. When a recipe is a success, they do well and there are smiles all round, but they have also to suffer when something doesn't turn out quite as expected.

So my heartfelt thanks to all my guinea pigs and especially to the following who over the years have shared culinary secrets with me and given me recipes and ideas for kitchen suppers: my husband James; Jenny Fraser; Ingrid, Mike and Ros Danckwerts; Viviane Slaski; Valentine Bond; Monique Fabre; Lynda Johnson; Judy Peppitt; Suzy Junor; Angela Dewar Guttierez; Betty Cripps; Roseline Feijoo; Nuria Gonell Cusido; Margaret Knott; Maria-Antoinetta Pau; Wendy and Jeremy Swann; Gina Raggett; Manoush Yegyayan. Special thanks too to Tracey Scoffield for her wisdom and tact, and to all the unsung heroines – and heroes – at Faber and Faber; and to Sara Menguc for having faith in me.

Introduction

One of the most delightful things in the world is to sit round a table with three or four people you really like, sharing a meal, drinking some wine, exchanging ideas and enjoying a gossip. Yet for the busy cook this dream too often turns into a nightmare and just thinking about all the work involved can be thoroughly off-putting.

For me, the most enjoyable evenings are spent over a kitchen supper either in my own or in a friend's house. For the last couple of years we all seem to have stopped giving dinner parties and settled instead for this appealing alternative. Just hearing the words, 'Come round for a kitchen supper,' makes us feel relaxed. The idea suggests warmth, a family atmosphere and a shared intimacy, and above all we know that no one need feel guilty because one of us has been bustling around for days on end, making lists, shopping, planning, cooking and polishing silver.

We all sit in the kitchen. Sometimes we spend the whole evening there, beginning with drinks round the table, which does away with the agony of the pre-meal drinks session going on too long while the cook worries about the food being spoiled. At a kitchen supper, you don't have to interrupt the talk, all you do is start producing the meal.

Compared to a dinner party, kitchen suppers are much more flexible. There's no reason why you should always feel obliged to serve three courses. Two will do, or even one provided there's enough of it, and there's no reason why you shouldn't turn to supermarkets and delicatessens for their ready-made courses, which nowadays can cover the whole meal. But if you do this too often you are definitely missing some of the fun and pleasure of feeding your friends, because it is immensely rewarding to offer things you have made yourself. It makes them feel loved and for you, one of the most satisfying moments is when everyone tells you how delicious something is and you can bask in the praise knowing it only took a few minutes to prepare.

I'd like to think you will use my ideas to set your own imagination going. Because planning a meal takes time and is sometimes daunting I have set the suppers out in complete menus, but don't feel obliged to follow me slavishly; chop, change and shuffle them about. If you are so inclined, leave out the starter and serve bought nibbles instead, and if you don't want to make a dessert, there's no reason why you shouldn't provide cheese and fruit in its place.

In planning the menus I have tried to get away from the idea that every main course must invariably be accompanied by two or three vegetables. This is a very English idea. Other countries do things differently. For example, a meal often begins with a vegetable or salad starter, and bread – whether it is wholemeal, French, Italian or naan – takes the place of potatoes or rice. However, I generally offer ideas for accompaniments which you can follow or not, depending on your timetable and own inclinations.

I've roamed around the cooking of many countries collecting ideas and trying them out. My criteria has been good food that is simple to prepare. None of the dishes is difficult to do and none takes hours of work. Throughout the book I have indicated where things can be prepared ahead of time if this suits your schedule, though if you prefer most can be put together on the evening itself. However, there are a few dishes which must be made in advance and this has been specified.

My choice of dishes has obviously been influenced by my own tastes and experiences. I have lived in the Middle East and nowadays spend part of each year in France, and both play a part in my cooking. I like to flavour food with herbs and spices and at times have a passion for garlic. But although I like exotic fare, I don't despise British traditions, and have given plenty of space to some of the best of our unequalled range of imaginative puddings and desserts. To make the menus instantly comprehensible, I have given the recipes English names, but usually their foreign name is included in the text.

Nowadays so much food is imported that we don't really have to worry too much about what is going to be available when we are planning a meal. However, it is more economical as well as immensely pleasing to eat things as they appear throughout the year, so I have arranged the menus in groups under the headings of the seasons, which means that none of the menus is alarmingly costly. However, feel free to break this mould if you wish – but whether you buy seasonally or not, it is always worth going for fresh, good quality ingredients.

I've followed our English custom and given quantities for four. I think this is a good number for a kitchen supper but of course if you invite more, just increase the principal ingredients. And there's no reason why the menus cannot be adapted to a candle-lit evening for two. Seasonings are always a question of taste and should be adjusted accordingly. No special cooking pots or utensils are called for, although when I'm in a hurry I could not do without my food processor or my very sharp pair of kitchen shears. Sometimes I like to use a mortar and pestle and a mouli-légumes. I also favour cast-iron pans and casseroles – especially useful is a shallow gratin dish – not only are they efficient, but in certain recipes when the food must be cooked on top of the stove before going into the oven, they save time and washing-up.

At the end of the book I have included a few extras and some useful sundries like mayonnaise, garlic breads and breadcrumbs. Here you'll find ideas for dips and bites, alcoholic drinks and fruits, which can be made at odd moments and will add that extra something to the evening, making your friends feel cosseted.

I have really enjoyed writing this book, discovering dishes and trying them out on friends and family, who in their turn have shared their ideas with me. I do hope that your kitchen suppers will be just as much fun, for that is what cooking and entertaining should be all about.

Jenny Baker, London, 1992

Spring

Spring Menu 1
Brown shrimps
Stir-fried chicken with ginger
Green salad with croûtons
Syllabub

Spring Menu 2
Raw vegetables with herb cheese
Trout in puff pastry
Cider ice

Spring Menu 3
Asparagus
Guinea fowl with spring vegetables and mushrooms
Gooseberry or rhubarb fool

Spring Menu 4
Sugar peas with lemon and chive sauce
Chilli baked fish
Marmalade pancakes

Spring Menu 5
Artichokes with anchovy butter
Rabbit in packets
Almond crumble

Spring Menu 6
Mustard roes on toast
Baked lamb chops with potatoes
Italian chocolate hazelnut cake

Spring Menu 7
Anchovy toasts
Duckling with glazed turnips
Whim-wham

Spring Menu 8
Spinach soup
Fish pie with puff-pastry crust
New potatoes and mange-tout
Baked bananas and oranges

Spring Menu 9
Oranges with artichoke hearts
Roast spring chicken with olive paste
Fried new potatoes
Rhubarb pie

Spring Menu 10
Hearts of palm
Spiced roast lamb
Potato and leek casserole
Poor Knights of Windsor

Spring Menu 11
New carrot and beetroot salad
Salmon kedgeree
Buttered crusty pears

Spring Menu 12
Quail eggs with cold meats
Fresh pasta with spring vegetables
Chocolate cream

Spring Menu 1

Brown shrimps
Stir-fried chicken with ginger
Green salad with croûtons
Syllabub

Small brown shrimps appear in spring on the fishmonger's slab. They are cheap and delicious. Pile them just as they are into a bowl; there's no need to peel them, and the gourmet eats the lot, head, shells, legs and all. If shrimps are unobtainable, buy prawns instead, which look very dramatic arranged on a long platter – these are shelled by everyone at table, so provide a bowl for the debris. Offer home-made mayonnaise (see p. 184), or a good commercial variety, and plenty of brown bread and butter. Cut the bread thinly, or simply put the loaf and a bowl of softened unsalted butter on the table and let everyone cut and butter their own slices. Be generous with fingerbowls and napkins.

Stir-frying is one of the quickest and most delicious ways of cooking chicken breasts. They are cut into fine strips and marinated in lemon juice, for the whole day if you like but at least an hour ahead. They are then tossed in a wok or large frying pan for a matter of minutes before being sprinkled with chopped fresh ginger, sesame seeds, garlic and parsley. Serve with a simple green salad with croûtons, plenty of crusty French bread and, if appetites are hearty, plain rice or a mixture of black and white rice (see p. 92).

Syllabub, which dates from the eighteenth century is simply cream whipped with lemon juice and alcohol and is as delicious as its name. It can be made at any time throughout the year but is particularly good in spring, when cream is at its best. Make it a day or two or even more ahead and store it in a cool place. I've read it separates if refrigerated, but I have not found this to be so.

Brown Shrimps

1.2 litres (2 pints) brown
  shrimps
mayonnaise

brown bread
100 g (4 oz) unsalted butter

To serve: Put shrimps in a bowl, the mayonnaise in another, and either thinly sliced buttered brown bread on a plate, or a loaf of wholemeal on a board and the butter in a third bowl.

Stir-fried Chicken with Ginger

4 boned chicken breasts,
  skinned
2 lemons, one quartered
freshly milled mixed or black
  pepper
2 tablespoons cornflour
salt
2–3 tablespoons olive or
  groundnut oil

sprinkling of soy sauce
1–2 teaspoons finely chopped
  fresh ginger
1 tablespoon sesame seeds
1–2 cloves garlic, chopped
handful chopped parsley
loaf crusty French or Italian
  bread

Prepare at least one or several hours ahead: Cut the meat into thin strips approximately 5 mm ($\frac{1}{4}$ in) wide. Put them in a shallow glass or china dish, squeeze over the juice of one of the lemons, and season with pepper. Cover and leave to marinate in a cool place. (If in the fridge, remove one hour before cooking.)

To cook: Put cornflour into a plastic bag, and season with salt. Add the chicken pieces and shake to coat them all over. Heat the oil in a frying pan, add the chicken pieces and toss them over a high heat for one minute. Lower heat slightly and continue to cook for 2 or 3 minutes, turning them over and over until they feel springy when pressed and are turning golden. Sprinkle with soy sauce, add ginger, sesame seeds, garlic and parsley, and cook a moment or two more.

To serve: Turn the chicken on to a heated serving dish, garnish with the lemon quarters and serve the bread separately.

Green Salad with Croûtons

1 round lettuce
packet lamb's lettuce or
  watercress
¼ cucumber, finely sliced
handful parsley or chervil,
  chopped
2 or three tablespoons
  snipped chives

handful bread croûtons
  (see p. 183)
1 teaspoon Dijon mustard
1 teaspoon vinegar
salt
freshly milled black pepper
3 or 4 tablespoons olive oil

Can be done ahead of time: Wash and dry lettuce, break into pieces and put into a salad bowl with the lamb's lettuce or watercress. Add sliced cucumber, herbs and croûtons. Put mustard, vinegar, salt, pepper and oil into a screw-top jar.
To serve: Shake dressing and pour over lettuce, sprinkle with the croûtons. Mix at table.

Syllabub

120 ml (4 fl oz) dry white
  wine or dry cider
thinly pared rind and juice of
  1 lemon
2 tablespoons calvados, pear
  liqueur or brandy

50 g (2 oz) caster sugar
300 ml (½ pint) double cream
grated nutmeg
sponge or almond biscuits

Prepare one or two days ahead: Put wine or cider, lemon rind, lemon juice and spirit into a jug and leave overnight.
Next day: Strain liquid into a large mixing bowl, add sugar and stir until it has dissolved. Gradually stir in the cream and beat with a wire whisk or electric beater until it is thick and soft. Don't overbeat or it will curdle. Spoon into small glasses or ramekin dishes, cover and keep cool.
To serve: Top each with a little grated nutmeg and hand the biscuits separately.

Spring Menu 2

Raw vegetables with herb cheese
Trout in puff pastry
Cider ice

The herb cheese dip with which these raw vegetables are eaten comes from France where it is known as *claqueret lyonnais* or *cervelle de canut*, which translated literally means silk-weaver's brain, because the Lyons silk-weavers often ate it as their evening meal, not being able to afford the authentic delicacy. Whatever the origins, it makes a pleasant dip with a selection of raw vegetables and should be prepared at least 24 hours ahead to allow the cheese to absorb the flavours of wine, vinegar, olive oil, garlic and herbs. If you are in a hurry, with no time to make the cheese, then do as the Italians do and offer instead a bowl of extra virgin olive oil seasoned with salt and pepper.

The trout in puff pastry can be prepared several hours ahead if this suits your schedule. It uses trout fillets which are sold ready-prepared at fish counters, or ask the fishmonger to fillet two trout for you. You can use frozen puff pastry, divided into four, or simply go for ready-rolled sheets. These are 20 cm (8 in) square, so check that each fish fillet will fit. The trout are baked for 25 minutes until the pastry is golden. Serve with tiny new potatoes boiled in their jackets and steamed mange-tout (see p. 27).

The amber-coloured ice from Normandy makes a refreshing end to the meal. It can be made days ahead, but if there's no time, buy instead any good quality fruit-flavoured sorbet.

Raw Vegetables with Herb Cheese

225 g (8 oz) goat's or ewe's cheese

2 tablespoons crème fraîche (see p. 187)

2 tablespoons white wine

1 teaspoon white wine vinegar

2 teaspoons olive oil

2 cloves garlic, chopped

handful chopped parsley

handful chopped chives
salt
freshly milled black pepper
selection of 3 or 4 different
    raw vegetables such as
    spring onions, sprigs of
    cauliflower, radishes,

celery, quartered tomatoes,
strips of carrot, fennel,
sliced sweet peppers,
cucumber, etc.
handful each of black and
    green olives

Prepare at least 24 hours ahead: Mash the cheese and beat in all
the other ingredients, one at a time except the raw vegetables and
olives. Pile into a bowl, cover and refrigerate.
To serve: Remove from fridge at least 1 hour before serving. Put
the bowl in the centre of a dish or board and surround with the
raw vegetables and olives.

Trout in Puff Pastry

50 g (2 oz) butter, cut in
    small pieces
4 sheets ready-rolled frozen
    puff pastry or 225 g (8 oz)
    block, defrosted, divided
    into 4 and rolled out
4 fillets of pink trout
2 tablespoons chopped fennel,
    tarragon or dill
1 tablespoon chopped chives
    grated zest and juice of 1
    lemon

salt
cayenne pepper
1 egg, beaten

For the sauce:
    50 g (2 oz) butter
    3–4 tablespoons crème
    fraîche (see p. 187)
    squeeze of lemon juice
    1 tablespoon green pepper-
    corns

Can be prepared several hours ahead: Put a few small pieces of
butter down the centre of each square of pastry and lay a fillet of
fish on top. Add a sprinkling of chopped herbs, a grating of lemon
zest, a squeeze of lemon juice, salt and cayenne pepper and dot
with remaining butter. Brush the edges of the squares with beaten
egg. Fold the pastry over the fish to form a long parcel, pressing
the overlapping edges together so they are sealed. Lay the parcels
on a damp baking sheet with the folded edges underneath, and

brush all over with egg. If not cooking immediately, slide the baking sheet into a plastic bag and refrigerate until ready to cook (when it goes into the hot oven, the metal sheet heats in seconds and there is no danger that the base won't be cooked).

To cook: Heat the oven to Gas 6/400°F/200°C. Bake 25 minutes until the pastry is risen and golden.

To serve: Melt the butter in a small saucepan, stir in the crème fraîche, lemon juice and green peppercorns. Let it boil and pour into a warm jug. At table get everyone to slit their parcels open and pour in some sauce.

Cider Ice

300 ml (½ pint) water	1 tablespoon calvados,
100 g (4 oz) sugar	brandy or white rum
zest and juice of 1 lemon	2 eggs
pinch of cinnamon	almond biscuits or wafers
300 ml (½ pint) dry cider	

Prepare at least one and up to several days ahead: Put water, sugar, the grated lemon zest and the cinnamon into a saucepan and boil for 3 minutes. Allow to cool and strain into a shallow container. Add lemon juice and the cider. Freeze until almost set (2–3 hours). Break up with a fork until the crystals are like snow and stir in the spirit. Separate the eggs (reserve the yolks for another occasion). Beat the whites until stiff and fold in the iced mixture. Return to the freezer.

To serve: Remove from freezer 15 minutes before serving. Pile into tall glasses and serve the almond biscuits or wafers separately.

Spring Menu 3

Asparagus
Guinea fowl with spring vegetables
and mushrooms
Gooseberry or rhubarb fool

Asparagus is seldom cheap but it makes a child's play starter in spring and early summer. Ideally it should be cooked in an asparagus kettle, a tall narrow pot complete with its own wire basket. This allows the stalks to be submerged in the boiling water, while the heads stand free and cook in the steam. You can buy these kettles in kitchen shops but you could be lucky like me and find one at a boot or jumble sale. Before I discovered mine I improvised, using a tall, plastic cutlery drainer in a deep pan and making a hooded lid with kitchen foil. It works well. Asparagus is such a treat that it doesn't need tarting up at all – leave hollandaise to the experts. Simply serve it with melted butter, or the easy sauce given in Spring Menu 4 for sugar peas; or eat it cold with olive or walnut oil flavoured with lemon juice.

This French recipe for guinea fowl, *pintadeau aux légumes*, combines all sorts of interesting flavours, sweet-tasting early carrots and turnips, earthy mushrooms, lemon and tarragon with an underlying hint of nutmeg. The bird is braised for an hour and the mushrooms added towards the end. It needs no other accompaniment than plain boiled rice in which I sometimes bury one or two whole cloves of garlic.

Now is the time when the commons and hedgerows are laced with creamy elderflowers, and rhubarb followed by the first gooseberries arrives in the shops. Both of these fruits combined with the flowers make delicious fools with a delicate hint of muscat grapes. If there are none to pick, add a tablespoon or two of elderflower cordial or sweet fortified wine such as Beaumes de Venise. Make your fool 1–2 days ahead. Rhubarb is the easiest: the stewed fruit needs only to be mashed. Gooseberries are more of a problem but not if you have a mouli-légumes, in which case the fruit can be cooked whole and then put through it, leaving all the hard tops and tails behind. Otherwise, the fruit must be topped and tailed before it is cooked, but this chore is made easy with scissors. Alternatively, you can skip the whole business, and blend a jar of drained gooseberries preserved in light syrup with the crème fraîche and fromage frais, flavouring it with elder-flower cordial. Add only a little sugar, as there should be an agreeable sharpness.

Asparagus

750 g (1½ lb) asparagus   100 g (4 oz) butter
salt

Can be prepared several hours ahead: Wash asparagus, remove coarse fibres with a potato peeler and tie into 4 bundles.
To cook: Stand bundles upright in the basket, put into the saucepan and half-fill with water, add salt and bring to the boil. Boil, covered, until tender, 20–30 minutes, then drain. Melt the butter.
To serve: Remove string and serve the asparagus on a platter, with the melted butter in a bowl in the centre.

Guinea Fowl with Spring Vegetables and Mushrooms

1 guinea fowl
salt
freshly milled black pepper
grated nutmeg
4 tablespoons oil
100 g (4 oz) streaky bacon,
  chopped
1 white or other mild-
  flavoured onion, sliced
225 g (8 oz) carrots, sliced

225 g (8 oz) turnips, chopped
150 ml (¼ pint) dry white
  wine
50 g (2 oz) butter
225 g (8 oz) flat field
  mushrooms, sliced
juice of 1 lemon
2 or 3 sprigs fresh or
  ½ teaspoon dried tarragon

To cook: Season the inside of the guinea fowl with salt, pepper and grated nutmeg. Heat half the oil in a heavy-based casserole and brown the bird all over. Remove to a plate. Add the remaining oil, bacon, onion, carrots and turnips. Cover and cook gently for 10 minutes. Return the guinea fowl to the casserole, pour over the wine, season with salt and pepper, cover and simmer for 1 hour.

Meanwhile, heat the butter in another pan and add the mushrooms, lemon juice and tarragon. Cover and stew gently for 10 minutes. Add to the guinea fowl 10–15 minutes before the end of cooking time, or when you sit down to the starter.

To serve: Serve the bird on a warm dish surrounded by the vegetables and mushrooms. Boil the sauce hard for a few minutes to reduce and then pour into a sauce boat.

Gooseberry or Rhubarb Fool

450 g (1 lb) gooseberries or rhubarb

2 heads of elderflower, or 1–2 tablespoons elder-flower cordial or muscat wine

50–75 g (2–3 oz) caster or vanilla sugar (see p. 186)

150 ml (¼ pint) crème fraîche, (see p. 187)

150 ml (¼ pint) fromage frais grated lemon rind or nutmeg almond biscuits

Prepare one or two days ahead: Put gooseberries (topped and tailed if you have no mouli-légumes) or rhubarb, cut into 5 cm (2 in) lengths, into a saucepan without water and bring slowly to the boil. Simmer until soft, 5–15 minutes. Dunk the flowerheads, if using, in and out of the fruit several times and discard. Add sugar to taste: there should be a hint of tartness. Put the gooseberries through the mouli-légumes, or mash top and tailed fruit. (Rhubarb should be strained over a bowl to catch the juice, and then mashed.) Mix mashed fruit with the elderflower cordial or muscat wine, if using. Fold in the crème fraîche and fromage frais, mixing to achieve a marbled effect. (Rhubarb mixture may need thinning with a little of the strained juice.) Spoon the fool into small pots or glasses.

To serve: Sprinkle grated lemon rind or nutmeg over each and hand the biscuits separately.

Spring Menu 4

*Sugar peas with lemon
and chive sauce
Chilli baked fish
Marmalade pancakes*

Sugar peas are more familiarly known under their French alias, *mange-tout*. Although keen gardeners have grown them for a long time, it is only recently that they have been produced on a commercial scale. Now, they seem to be on sale almost all the year round, many being imported along with their plumper cousins, sugar snap peas, from Africa, which are likewise eaten pods and all. They make a wonderful vegetable, but to appreciate their unadulterated sweetness eat them as a first course, picking them up in the fingers and dipping them either into melted butter or in this creamy sauce sharpened with lemon juice and chives.

Almost any kind of firm fish steaks or fillets can be used for the main dish, which is put together very quickly either just before it goes into the oven or several hours ahead. This version is based on a Languedoc recipe, but there are variations on the theme from South America to the countries of the Mediterranean. Serve it with plain rice or mashed potatoes or, if there's just no time, bake some jacket potatoes for 1 hour in the oven on a shelf above the fish.

The pancake dessert is simplicity itself because it uses those excellent French crêpes sold in supermarkets – but of course if you are a dab hand at pancakes, there's nothing but the time involved to stop you making your own. They are filled with marmalade and curd cheese, pepped up with a dash of spirits and the result is quite something. Pancakes you buy are packed folded into four to form a triangle; to fill, just open them out into a semi-circle.

Sugar Peas with Lemon and Chive Sauce

450 g (1 lb) mange-tout
  (sugar peas)
salt
50 g (2 oz) butter
150 ml (¼ pint) clotted cream

or crème fraîche
  (see p. 187)
freshly milled black pepper
handful chopped chives
juice of ½ lemon

Can be done ahead: Top and tail the mange-tout and remove stringy bits.

To cook: Boil or steam mange-tout, seasoned with salt, for 5–10 minutes, until soft but still crunchy, then drain. Meanwhile, melt the butter in a small pan, add cream and stir until boiling. Season with the salt, pepper, chives and lemon juice.

To serve: Put mange-tout on a warm platter and the sauce in a bowl in the centre.

Chilli Baked Fish

4 fillets or steaks of firm
  white fish such as cod,
  haddock, coley, hake,
  halibut, etc.
1½ lemons
1 onion, finely chopped
2 cloves garlic, chopped
1 can Italian chopped
  tomatoes

1 teaspoon oregano or
  marjoram
2 whole red chillies
salt
freshly milled black pepper
2 handfuls breadcrumbs
  (see p. 183)
olive oil

Can be prepared several hours ahead: Oil a baking dish and lay the fish in it in a single layer. Sprinkle with the juice of the half lemon. Add onion and garlic. Pour over the canned tomatoes, spreading them evenly over the top. Add oregano, chillies, salt and pepper. Sprinkle with breadcrumbs. Slice the whole lemon and lay the slices down the middle. Sprinkle with the oil.

To cook: Heat the oven to Gas 6/400°F/200°C and bake for 40 minutes until hot and bubbling.

Marmalade Pancakes

4–6 pancakes
100 g (4 oz) curd cheese
4–6 tablespoons Seville
  orange marmalade
50 g (2 oz) muscovado sugar

25 g (1 oz) butter
juice of ½ orange
2 tablespoons whisky,
  brandy, calvados or rum

Can be prepared several hours ahead: Open each pancake into a semi-circle and spread with curd cheese and marmalade. Roll up and lay them side by side in a buttered oven-proof dish. Sprinkle with the sugar and dot with butter. Squeeze over orange juice. **To cook:** Heat the oven to Gas 5/375°F/190°C. Sprinkle with the spirit and bake for 5–10 minutes until hot through.

Spring Menu 5

Artichokes with anchovy butter
Rabbit in packets
Almond crumble

Eating artichokes is a matey business, which makes them a good choice for a kitchen supper. Here they are eaten hot, but if you prefer cook them ahead of time and serve them cold with a vinaigrette flavoured with a few chopped anchovies. If you decide to do this, cook them on the day because once cooked they gradually go black. Artichokes are perhaps no longer a mystery but if you've not prepared or eaten them before, this is what you do. Don't cut but break off the stalks and pull away the stringy fibres that grow into the heart. Soak the artichokes upside down for an hour, in salted water with a squeeze of lemon juice, to get rid of any insects. Before cooking, trim the stalk ends flat so they can stand upright. There's no need to trim the leaves. To test if they are cooked, pull off an outer leaf and bite the base (which is the only edible part). It should be soft – if not, continue cooking. Serve them well drained on individual plates. Everyone dismantles their own with their fingers by pulling off the leaves one by one, dipping the fleshy base into the sauce and arranging their discarded leaves as they wish around their plate. Finally the fibrous choke is cut away to reveal the succulent heart, which disappears all too quickly in 3 or 4 mouthfuls.

The main course follows a Provençal recipe, *lapin en paquets à la brignolaise*. Buy rabbit portions or a whole rabbit and ask your supplier to cut it into 8 for you. The pieces are then wrapped in bacon and cooked on a bed of tomatoes, flavoured with shallots, garlic and herbs. The dish can be assembled hours ahead of the meal if this is convenient, or all the preparations can be done just before it goes into the oven. It takes an hour to cook and goes beautifully with steamed or boiled potatoes dusted with parsley.

The almond crumble can be varied according to what fruit is available. I have used apples, dried apricots and bananas. It too can be assembled well ahead of time or just before it is cooked, depending on your schedule. It goes into the oven 20 minutes before the rabbit is ready and finishes cooking while this is being eaten. Right at the last moment it is covered with single cream which is absorbed by the topping and fruit to give a richly moist pudding.

Artichokes with Anchovy Butter

4 artichokes	100 g (4 oz) butter
salt	4 anchovy fillets, chopped
2 tablespoons lemon juice or	2 cloves garlic, chopped
vinegar	freshly milled black pepper

Prepare an hour or so ahead: Break off the stalks and trim the bases flat. Soak upside down in salted water with the lemon juice or vinegar.
To cook: Bring a large pan of salted water to the boil. Add the artichokes and boil for 30–40 minutes. Test by pulling off one of the lower leaves and tasting the fleshy part at its base. Drain well.
To serve: Melt the butter in a small pan with the anchovies and garlic, season with salt and pepper. Serve the artichokes on individual plates, the sauce in a bowl in the centre.

Rabbit in Packets

2 tablespoons olive oil
225 g (8 oz) shallots, chopped
1 rabbit cut into 8 pieces or
  900 g (2 lb) rabbit portions
4 cloves garlic, chopped
salt

freshly milled black pepper
8 rashers streaky bacon
1 can Italian chopped
  tomatoes
½ teaspoon dried thyme
handful chopped fresh parsley

Can be prepared several hours ahead: Heat the oil in a wide, flameproof gratin dish and fry the shallots gently until golden but not brown or they will be bitter. Meanwhile sprinkle each piece of rabbit with garlic, salt and pepper and wrap in a rasher of bacon. Pour the tomatoes over the shallots, sprinkle with thyme and season with salt and pepper. Lay the rabbit pieces on top.

To cook: Heat the oven to Gas 6/400°F/200°C. Bring the dish to the boil on top of the stove. Put into the oven and bake for 45 minutes, basting once or twice.

To serve: Sprinkle over the parsley and serve from the cooking dish.

Almond Crumble

12 dried apricots
100 g (4 oz) flour
50 g (2 oz) ground almonds
75 g (3 oz) soft brown sugar
150 g (6 oz) softened butter
450 g (1 lb) Cox's or other

eating apples, peeled, cored
  and sliced
2 bananas, sliced
½ teaspoon cinnamon
grated nutmeg
single cream or smetana

Can be prepared several hours ahead: Put apricots in a bowl and just cover with boiling water; leave to soak for 30 minutes. Mix flour, almonds, sugar and butter either in a food processor or by hand to make a crumble topping. Put the sliced apples into a buttered dish, add bananas and finally the apricots with their soaking liquid. Sprinkle with the cinnamon and nutmeg and spread the crumble topping over the fruit.

To cook: Heat the oven to Gas 6/400°F/200°C and bake for

25–30 minutes. At this point it can be kept warm in the turned-off oven.

To serve: Serve cream or smetana separately.

Spring Menu 6

Mustard roes on toast
Baked lamb chops with potatoes
Italian chocolate hazelnut cake

The herring roes for this starter are gently fried for a few minutes with mustard and cayenne pepper, before being dusted with parsley, piled into a bowl and surrounded by quartered lemons. Get someone to make the toast while you do the roes and make sure the butter is taken out of the fridge an hour or so ahead so that it is not rock hard. Offer cocktail sticks too so that everyone can spear pieces of roe on to the toast.

The recipe for the lamb chops is based on the Languedoc dish, *bombine*. Like most country dishes there are as many variations as there are cooks. This one containing bacon, potatoes, olives and tomatoes is a complete meal in a pot and can be made with lamb or pork. The chops are baked in a dish with all the other ingredients, so start preparations an hour or so before the meal. It only needs a green salad and French bread to accompany it.

The Italian-inspired chocolate cake is one of those miracles which need no cooking. It is moist and gooey and extremely rich. Make it the day before and cover it with whipped cream (flavoured with amaretto, rum or brandy) and grated chocolate just before serving. You can buy roasted, chopped hazelnuts but if not obtainable, roast hazelnuts under the grill and grind them, not too finely, in a food mill.

Mustard Roes on Toast

50 g (2 oz) butter
1 teaspoon Dijon mustard
cayenne pepper
350 g (12 oz) soft herring
   roes, cut in bite-sized pieces

handful chopped parsley
2 lemons, quartered
8 slices toast
bowl of unsalted butter
cocktail sticks

To cook: Melt butter in a frying pan, stir in mustard and season with cayenne pepper. Gently cook the roes for 3 or 4 minutes, turning once. Sprinkle with parsley and pile them into a warm bowl. Stand the bowl on a serving dish and garnish with the quartered lemons. Put the toast in a rack or on a plate and hand round the butter and cocktail sticks separately.

Baked Lamb Chops with Potatoes

2 tablespoons olive oil
4 lamb chump chops or
   escalopes
2 onions, chopped
750 g (1½ lb) potatoes, peeled
   and sliced
1 can Italian chopped
   tomatoes
½ teaspoon dried thyme

bay leaf
salt
freshly milled black pepper
2 cloves garlic, chopped
300 ml (½ pint) approx. stock
   or water
8 slices streaky bacon
handful black olives

To cook: Heat the oven to Gas 5/375°F/190°C. Heat the oil in a wide flameproof casserole or gratin dish and brown the chops on both sides. Remove to a plate. Add onions and fry until golden. Lay half the potatoes on top of the onions and then the chops. Pour on the tomatoes and add thyme, bay leaf, salt, pepper and garlic. Cover with the remaining potatoes and season again with salt and pepper. Pour in just enough stock or water to barely cover. Lay the bacon rashers on top. Bake for 45 minutes. Add the olives and cook for a further 15 minutes.

Italian Chocolate Hazelnut Cake

225 g (8 oz) rich tea biscuits
150 g (6 oz) softened butter
3 eggs, separated
150 g (6 oz) drinking
  chocolate powder
100 g (4 oz) chopped, roasted
  hazelnuts

150 ml (¼ pint) double cream,
  whipped
2 teaspoons amaretto, rum or
  brandy
25–50 g (1–2 oz) plain
  chocolate, grated

Make one day ahead: Line base and sides of a sandwich tin, 20 cm (8 in) in diameter with a removable base, with greaseproof paper. Break up the biscuits and crush them in a food processor – or put them into a plastic bag and crush with a rolling pin. Put the softened butter into a mixing bowl and beat in the egg yolks. Beat in the chocolate powder until the mixture is smooth. Mix in the crushed biscuits and hazelnuts. Beat the three egg whites until they hold their shape, and fold into the mixture. Pile it into the cake tin, smooth the top and cover with a circle of greaseproof paper. Put a well-fitting plate or lid on top and weight it down with something heavy, like a flat-iron or can. Refrigerate until next day.

To serve: Remove top circle of greaseproof paper, carefully turn the cake on to a serving dish and remove remaining paper. Cover with whipped cream flavoured with the amaretto, rum or brandy, and the grated chocolate.

Spring Menu 7

Anchovy toasts
Duckling with glazed turnips
Whim-wham

Anchovies, olive oil and a loaf of French bread are the ingredients for these appetizers, the *quichets* of Provence. They can be prepared hours ahead and then go into the oven for a few minutes. Eat them with pre-supper drinks, sitting round the table.

There are several different French recipes for duckling with turnips, and this one comes from Burgundy, *caneton de Jarnoy*. Ducks have a thick layer of fat under the skin: to release this, the duckling is first pricked all over and then browned slowly and thoroughly, causing most of the fat to run out. The fat is then discarded, and the bird is braised in a little wine on a bed of carrots, onions and shallot. It emerges sweet and succulent, and very tender. Meanwhile, the turnips are caramelized in butter and sugar and are served surrounding the duckling. Small green peas, the *petits pois* that come out of a can, make a pretty accompaniment.

This supper had been going to end with junket, which for me goes back to the days when my grandmother served it with home-made jam and huge dollops of Devonshire cream. The milk, 600 ml (1 pint) of it, was gently heated to blood temperature and stirred into a bowl standing in the larder, containing a tablespoon of caster sugar and one of brandy. Once the sugar had dissolved, a teaspoon of rennet was stirred in and then the mixture was left undisturbed until set, about 2 hours. Just before serving it was dusted with freshly grated nutmeg. It used to be so easy, but nowadays rennet is impossible to find, at least where I live. At one time it was sold in every chemist's and many grocer's – you might be lucky and have a good delicatessen who stocks it. So instead I have chosen an equally old English dessert, whim-wham: little trifles flavoured with elderflower cordial or sherry and glacé ginger, which should be made several hours ahead or the day before.

Anchovy Toasts

100 g (4 oz) canned
  anchovies, chopped
2 cloves garlic, chopped
2 teaspoons red wine vinegar

4 tablespoons olive oil
freshly milled black pepper
1 long French loaf
olive oil for sprinkling

Can be prepared several hours ahead: Put the anchovies, garlic and vinegar into a food processor, or mortar, and blend well. Beat in the olive oil and season with pepper.

To cook: Heat oven to Gas 6/400°F/200°C. Cut the loaf in half lengthwise, flatten it slightly, sprinkle with olive oil and spread with the anchovy paste. Cut into serving portions and put on to a baking sheet. Bake at the top of the oven for 5–10 minutes, until bubbling and golden.

Duckling with Glazed Turnips

1 plump duckling
2 tablespoons olive oil
2 onions, chopped
1 shallot, chopped
225 g (8 oz) carrots, chopped
150 ml (¼ pint) white wine,
  stock or water
sprig of thyme or ½ teaspoon
  dried

bay leaf
salt
freshly milled black pepper
50 g (2 oz) butter
750 g (1½ lb) young,
  even-sized turnips
1 teaspoon caster sugar
1 tablespoon water

To cook: Prick the skin of the bird all over with a fork. Heat the oil in a flameproof casserole and brown the duckling all over on a medium heat, turning as necessary. This will take about 20 minutes. Remove the duckling to a plate and pour away all but 1 tablespoon of the fat. Put in the onions, shallot and carrots and cook them gently for about 5 minutes. Put the duckling on top, pour in the wine, stock or water, add the thyme and bay leaf and season with salt and pepper. Cover and simmer for 1 hour.

Meanwhile, melt the butter in another pan, add the turnips and cook them gently until beginning to turn golden, turning them from time to time. Sprinkle over the sugar, season with salt and pepper and add 1 tablespoon of water. Cover and simmer on a low heat for 45 minutes until the duckling is done.

To serve: Before serving the starter, turn off the heat under the casserole. This will allow time for the duckling to rest and the flesh to firm up. Serve it on a warm dish, surrounded by the vegetables in which it was cooked and the turnips. Strain the sauce into a sauceboat.

Whim-Wham

12 sponge fingers
4 dessertspoons elderflower
   cordial or sherry
300 ml (½ pint) double cream,
   whipped

chopped, roasted hazelnuts
chopped glacé ginger

Make several hours or a day ahead: Line 4 individual dishes or little pots with the sponge fingers, breaking them to fit. Sprinkle over the elderflower cordial or sherry. Pile whipped cream on top and sprinkle with hazelnuts and ginger.

 ## Spring Menu 8

Spinach soup
Fish pie with a puff-pastry crust
New potatoes and mange-tout
Baked bananas and oranges

Spinach soup, dark green in colour, its sweetness subtly complemented with the taste of bacon, can be made well ahead, but it's so easy that it can just as well be done in the run-up to the meal. The stock can be made with a cube, but it's even better if you have some real chicken or vegetable stock – the latter could simply be the water in which some other vegetable was cooked.

   Fish pie seems an obvious choice for a kitchen supper, yet it can be quite a chore, involving several cooking processes. This version aims to reduce the work. Choose firm white fish such as coley, hake, rock salmon (dogfish), haddock or cod, using all one sort or a mixture of two or three. The fish is first gently poached in water flavoured with cider – use strong dry cider, anything sweeter is just cloying – and the resulting stock is used to make the sauce, which forms part of the filling for the pie. Some people like to replace some of the stock with single cream. To give added colour and more flavour, I include a can of red salmon but this could be 225 g (8 oz) smoked fish such as haddock or mackerel or, if you're feeling rich, you could throw in the equivalent weight of prawns or scallops. If you have a square pie dish, use a sheet of ready-rolled puff pastry, otherwise buy a block and roll it to the required shape. Accompany the pie with boiled potatoes and steamed mange-tout, saving on the washing-up by steaming the mange-tout over the potatoes and serving them in the same dish.

The meal ends with a melting mixture of bananas and oranges, which can be prepared an hour or two ahead and goes into the oven when you sit down to eat.

Spinach Soup

25 g (1 oz) butter
100 g (4 oz) streaky bacon, chopped
1 onion, chopped
225 g (8 oz) frozen spinach
225 g (8 oz) potatoes, quartered

1 litre (1¾ pints) chicken or vegetable stock
grated nutmeg
salt
freshly milled black pepper
100 g (4 oz) croûtons (see p. 183)

Can be prepared up to a day or two ahead: Melt the butter in a large pan, add the bacon pieces and onion and fry until golden. Add the frozen spinach and cook until it softens. Add the quartered potatoes (no need to peel) and stock. Season with grated nutmeg, salt and pepper, cover and simmer for 20–30 minutes until the potatoes are soft. Put through a food processor or mouli-légumes.

To serve: Heat the soup and serve the croûtons separately.

Fish Pie with a Puff-pastry Crust

750 g (1½ lb) fillets of white
    fish
300 ml (½ pint) strong dry
    cider
300 ml (½ pint) water,
    approx.
bay leaf
sprig of parsley
½ teaspoon dried thyme
50 g (2 oz) butter
2 heaped tablespoons flour

handful chopped fresh fennel
    and parsley and 1 table-
    spoon capers, *or* chopped
    coriander leaves and a
    thread or two of saffron
pinch cayenne pepper
salt
225 g (8 oz) can red salmon,
    chopped
225 g (8 oz) puff pastry
1 egg, beaten

Can be prepared up to a day ahead: Lay the fish in a saucepan, pour over the cider or wine and enough water to cover, and add the bay leaf, sprig of parsley and thyme. Bring to the boil, cover and simmer for 5–8 minutes until the fish turns opaque. Drain the fish in a colander. Strain the liquid into a measuring jug and return 450 ml (¾ pint) of it to the saucepan. Add the butter, sprinkle in the flour and bring to the boil over a medium heat, beating constantly with a wire whisk to prevent lumps forming. As the sauce thickens, lower the heat and simmer for 2 minutes, still beating. Add fennel, parsley and capers (or coriander and saffron) and season to taste with cayenne pepper and salt. Remove from the heat. Butter a pie dish. Use your fingers to break up the fish, discarding skin and bones, and put it into the dish. Add the chopped, canned salmon, including skin and bones which will dissolve as the pie cooks. Pour over the sauce and set aside to cool.

To cook: Heat the oven to Gas 6/400°F/200°C. Roll out the pastry, if necessary, to fit the dish. Lay the pastry on top of the pie dish and tuck corners and edges in. Brush with the beaten egg. Put the pie on a baking sheet and bake for 30–35 minutes.

New Potatoes and Mange-tout

900 g (2 lb) small new potatoes, scrubbed, not peeled
salt
sprig of mint

450 g (1 lb) mange-tout, topped and tailed
25 g (1 oz) butter
handful chopped chervil or parsley

To cook: Put potatoes into boiling salted water with the mint and simmer, covered, for 10 minutes. Put the mange-tout into a steamer and stand it over the potatoes. Cover, and continue cooking for a further 10 minutes.
To serve: Drain the potatoes and serve the 2 vegetables arranged in the same dish. Top with dabs of butter and sprinkle with chervil or parsley.

Baked Bananas and Oranges

4 bananas, cut in half lengthwise
juice of 1 lemon
2 oranges, peeled and sliced
4 tablespoons soft brown sugar
1 teaspoon ground cinnamon

grated nutmeg
50 g (2 oz) butter
150 ml (¼ pint) single cream
2 tablespoons calvados, brandy or pear liqueur
2 or 3 tablespoons chopped, roasted hazelnuts

Can be prepared an hour or two ahead: Put bananas into a buttered dish. Sprinkle with lemon juice. Cover with orange slices (discarding outer pith and pips). Add sugar, cinnamon and nutmeg and dot with the butter.
To cook: Heat the oven to Gas 5/375°F/190°C. Bake the bananas for 10 minutes. Pour over the cream, sprinkle with the spirit and top with the hazelnuts. Bake for a further 10 minutes. Will keep warm in the turned-off oven.

Spring Menu 9

Oranges with artichoke hearts
Roast spring chicken
with olive paste
Fried new potatoes
Rhubarb pie

This quick to assemble, Italian-inspired starter, *arance e carciofi*, can be prepared in minutes, but the oranges need to be marinated in a little sugar for at least half an hour. I suggest you buy small artichoke hearts preserved in oil, *carcifioni*, which are fairly widely sold in delicatessens and some supermarkets. If you can't get them, use the canned variety instead.

A spring chicken will feed 2 people, but if appetites are huge, allow one each. They can be spatchcocked – split down the middle, flattened and grilled like the quail in Summer menu 4 – but roasting requires less attention. In this recipe a definite but unobtrusive flavour of olives is given by spreading the birds with Italian black olive paste, sold in delicatessens and some supermarkets. Or try instead a simple alternative and spread the birds with a herb-flavoured mustard. They can be prepared well ahead and roasted just before the meal. Serve them with a green salad and this Italian recipe for fried new potatoes, *patate arrostite*. Use small, even-sized potatoes (there's no need to peel them) and cook them in a wide, lidded pan in which they will sit in one layer.

Pink-stalked forced rhubarb comes into the shops in early spring and is infinitely nicer than the coarser summer variety which used to be stuffed into us when we were children. It makes a lovely pie which can be prepared hours ahead and baked at the same time as the chicken. It's nicest warm, so take it out of the oven while you eat the main course. Make sure you trim away all the rhubarb leaves – which are poisonous – and the discoloured base ends. As you cut it discard any stringy bits but don't peel it, because if you do it will lose its beautiful colour as it cooks. The pernod or pastis adds an elusive flavour of fennel, but it is equally delicious with a dash of elderflower cordial.

Oranges with Artichoke Hearts

2 oranges
1 tablespoon sugar
1 jar or can artichoke hearts
freshly milled black pepper
handful chopped parsley

if using artichokes in brine:
  1 clove garlic, chopped, and
  2–3 tablespoons olive or
  walnut oil

Prepare half an hour or several hours ahead: Peel oranges, removing all the pith. Quarter and slice into a shallow serving bowl and sprinkle with the sugar. If using artichoke hearts in brine drain them well, sprinkle with chopped garlic and the olive or walnut oil, and set aside until just before the meal.

To serve: Quarter the artichoke hearts and pour over the oil in the jar or the oil in which they have been marinating. Carefully mix them with the oranges. Season with pepper and garnish with the chopped parsley.

Roast Spring Chicken with Olive Paste

2–4 spring chickens
1–2 cloves garlic, chopped
black olive paste or mustard
1 teaspoon dried oregano
freshly milled mixed or black
  pepper

olive oil
bunch of watercress
1–2 lemons quartered

Can be prepared ahead: Cut each chicken completely in half lengthwise, using kitchen shears or a sharp knife. Oil a shallow earthenware gratin dish and lay them in it skin-side up. Sprinkle with the garlic and spread each bird with olive paste or mustard and sprinkle over the oregano and pepper. Cover and leave in a cool place until ready to cook.

To cook: Heat the oven to Gas 6/400°F/200°C. Sprinkle the chicken halves with olive oil and bake for 35–40 minutes, basting once half-way through.

To serve: Garnish with watercress and lemon quarters.

Fried New Potatoes

50 g (2 oz) butter
1 tablespoon olive oil
750 g (1½ lb) new potatoes
sprig of fresh rosemary,
    optional

salt
freshly milled black pepper

To cook: Heat the butter and oil in the pan, add the potatoes and shake to coat them all over. Add the sprig of rosemary. Cover and cook on a fairly low heat, shaking the pan from time to time, until they are crisp and golden, about 30 minutes. Serve sprinkled with salt and pepper.

Rhubarb Pie

1 sheet or 225 g (8 oz) puff
    pastry
750 g (1½ lb) rhubarb, cut in
    lengths of about 5 cm (2 in)
100 g (4 oz) soft brown sugar
½ teaspoon ground ginger
¼ teaspoon cinnamon

¼ teaspoon nutmeg
2 teaspoons pastis or pernod,
    or elderflower cordial
beaten egg white
1 tablespoon caster sugar
smetana, pouring cream or
    yogurt

Can be prepared several hours ahead: Defrost pastry. Put the rhubarb into a pie dish. Sprinkle over the brown sugar, ginger, cinnamon, nutmeg and pastis. Roll out the pastry to fit (if not ready-rolled). Cover the rhubarb with the pastry, tucking in the corners.
To cook: Heat the oven to Gas 6/400°F/200°C. Brush the pastry with the egg white, sprinkle with the caster sugar and bake for 35–40 minutes until top is golden. Remove from oven to cool.
To serve: Serve warm with the smetana, cream or yogurt, served separately.

Spring Menu 10

Hearts of palm
Spiced roast lamb
Potato and leek casserole
Poor Knights of Windsor

The taste of canned hearts of palm from Brazil is something between artichokes and asparagus. They are obtainable in some supermarkets, otherwise look for them in delicatessens. They go well with a sharp lime or lemon dressing, and in this salad their whiteness is complemented by red tomatoes, black olives and the fresh green of herbs. One of the dressing ingredients is *pesto*, the Italian basil sauce sold in jars. If unobtainable, you could use mustard instead. Prepare the salad at least 2 hours ahead to allow the flavours to develop.

The spiced roast lamb is marinated overnight with garlic, cumin, coriander and paprika. Next day it is roasted for about an hour, depending on the weight, and served with a wine gravy and a potato and leek gratin. If I am feeding garlic lovers, I pander to them by breaking up a whole head or two of garlic into cloves which I simmer unpeeled in a covered pan for about 20 minutes, until they are soft. These are served in a small bowl for everyone to help themselves, and squeeze out the sweet purée with their forks.

The meal ends with a delightful nursery pudding that turns up all over the place with only slight regional variations. Basically it is day-old bread dipped in a mixture of eggs and milk, fried until golden and served sprinkled with cinnamon and icing sugar. It's deliciously simple. We call it Poor Knights of Windsor, the French flavour it with rum and call it *pain perdu*; to the Dutch it is *wentelteefjes* and in Spain it is known as *torrijas*, where oil, rather than butter, is the frying medium. Whatever its name and origins, your chief concern is to make sure you have some day-old French bread.

Hearts of Palm

juice of ½ lime or lemon
2 teaspoons *pesto* (or 1 tea-
    spoon Dijon mustard)
6 tablespoons olive oil
2 garlic cloves, chopped
salt

freshly milled black pepper
2 cans hearts of palm
2 or 3 tomatoes, chopped
handful black olives
handful chives, chopped
handful parsley, chopped

At least 2 hours ahead: Make dressing by shaking the lime or
lemon juice in a screw-top jar with the *pesto* or mustard, olive oil,
garlic, salt and pepper. Rinse and slice the palm hearts quite
thinly diagonally, discarding any woody pieces. Put slices into a
china or glass dish and pour over the dressing.
To serve: Garnish with the chopped tomatoes, olives and fresh
herbs.

Spiced Roast Lamb

1.5 kg (3 lb) approx. leg of
    lamb
2 cloves garlic, cut in slivers
2 tablespoons coriander seeds
2 teaspoons cumin seeds

2 teaspoons paprika
freshly milled black pepper
olive oil
150 ml (¼ pint) red or dry
    white wine

Day before or several hours ahead: Put the meat into a dish and
cut slits in it with a pointed knife. Insert the slivers of garlic into
the slits. Crush the coriander and cumin seeds and mix with the
paprika. Spread this mixture over the joint. Sprinkle with the
pepper and set aside in a cool place for the spices to impregnate
the meat.
To cook: Heat the oven to Gas 6/400°F/200°C. Put the meat into a
roasting tin and sprinkle liberally with olive oil. If you like lamb
to be pink, roast for approximately 1 hour, basting occasionally;
if you prefer it to be well-done, allow an extra 20 minutes. Before
eating the starter, remove the meat from oven, put it on a serving
dish, return it to the oven and reduce the temperature to
Gas ½/250°F/120°C. (This allows time for the meat to contract,
making it easier to carve.)

To serve: Pour off most of the fat from the roasting tin, stir in the wine and let it bubble for a few minutes. Pour into a gravy boat.

Potato and Leek Casserole

50 g (2 oz) butter
450 g (1 lb) leeks, sliced,
  green ends discarded
900 g (2 lb) potatoes, peeled
  and sliced
450 ml (¾ pint) water
bay leaf

1 teaspoon dried thyme
salt
freshly milled black pepper
pinch of nutmeg
1–2 tablespoons snipped
  chives

To cook: Heat the oven to Gas 6/400°F/200°C. Melt half the butter in a medium-sized flameproof casserole and add the leeks. Cover and let them sweat for 5–10 minutes. Remove lid, mix in the potatoes and add the water, bay leaf and thyme. Season with salt, pepper and the nutmeg. Bring to the boil, dot with the remaining butter and put into the oven to bake for 40 minutes. (The casserole can be left in the oven with the meat while the starter is eaten.)
To serve: Sprinkle with the snipped chives.

Poor Knights of Windsor

2 eggs
100 g (4 oz) caster or vanilla
  sugar (see p. 186)
grated rind of ½ lemon
cinnamon
300 ml (½ pint) milk
100 g (4 oz) concentrated
  butter (see p. 187)

8–12 slices day-old French
  bread, 1 cm (½ in)
icing sugar
jam or whipped cream, or
  both

Prepare one hour ahead of time: In a shallow dish, beat the eggs with the sugar, lemon rind and a pinch of cinnamon. Beat in the milk. Leave to stand for 1 hour.

To fry: Melt the butter in a heavy-based frying pan. Dip the bread slices into the milk mixture and fry them until golden on both sides, transferring them to a warm plate.

To serve: Sprinkle with cinnamon and icing sugar and offer the jam and/or whippd cream separately.

Spring Menu 11

New carrot and beetroot salad
Salmon kedgeree
Buttered crusty pears

In spring the new carrots appear, looking especially appealing when sold in bunches still attached to their feathery leaves. Make the most of their sweet flavour by washing and grating them, and setting them on a platter surrounded by the dramatic crimson of sliced beetroot. This simple combination makes a refreshing starter before the rich main course. Most beetroot is now sold ready-cooked in a sealed plastic wrapping. Open it carefully, as the juice dyes everything it touches – though it easily washes off your hands and chopping board. Serve the salad with plenty of garlic bread.

Before the days of farmed salmon, spring was the beginning and the most expensive period of the salmon season, so dishes like kedgeree provided economical ways of savouring it. Nowadays, salmon is nearly always available, but for me this is the time of the year when I most enjoy it. Kedgeree, which is a Raj adaptation of an Indian dish *kicheri*, can be made with other kinds of fish, most notably smoked haddock. Some of the preparation can be done ahead, but really it is an ideal choice for supper on an evening when you're feeling relaxed and happy, and like the idea of chatting and cooking in front of the guests. Filleted salmon is to be found at the fish counters of supermarkets, but if not available, buy steaks or ask the fishmonger for a whole piece. Serve with a bowl of watercress or lamb's lettuce.

This lovely Norman way of cooking comice pears provides a

sweet ending to the meal. The same method can be used for other fruit, such as apples, peaches, apricots or plums. Pieces of brioche are dipped in melted butter, sprinkled with sugar and piled with slices of fruit which are sprinkled with lemon juice and more sugar. The dish then goes into the oven until the outer edges of the brioche are crisp and brown with caramelized sugar, while the centre with its topping of fruit remains meltingly soft. If you can't find a brioche loaf, buy a milk loaf instead, or failing that use any good white bread.

New Carrot and Beetroot Salad

225 g (8 oz) new carrots, peeled and grated
225 g (8 oz) cooked beetroot, peeled and sliced
1 clove garlic, chopped
6 tablespoons olive oil
1 tablespoon lemon juice
1 teaspoon mustard
salt
freshly milled black pepper

3 or 4 anchovy fillets, chopped
2–3 tablespoons chopped parsley
1 orange, peel and pith removed, chopped
1 tablespoon chopped fennel or chives
garlic bread
(see p. 184)

Can be prepared several hours ahead: Put the grated carrot in the centre of a shallow dish or bowl. Surround it with the slices of beetroot. In a screw-top jar mix the chopped garlic, olive oil, lemon juice, mustard, salt and pepper and sprinkle this dressing over the salad.

To serve: Sprinkle the chopped anchovies and parsley over the beetroot. Arrange chopped orange on top of the carrot (discarding pips) and sprinkle over the fennel or chives. Serve with garlic bread or *bruschetta*.

Salmon Kedgeree

450–700 g (1–1½ lb) salmon
   fillets
water to cover
juice of ½ lemon
bay leaf
sprig of parsley
8 peppercorns
3 eggs
250 g (8 oz) long-grain rice
salt
50 g (2 oz) butter

1 onion, chopped
1 teaspoon dried oregano
freshly grated nutmeg
3 or 4 tablespoons crème
   fraîche (see p. 187)
salt
freshly milled black pepper
handful parsley, chopped
2 or 3 tablespoons snipped
   chives
1 teaspoon paprika

Can be prepared several hours or one day ahead: Lay the salmon in a saucepan, cover with cold water and add the lemon juice, bay leaf, parsley and peppercorns. Bring slowly to the boil. If cooking ahead, cover the pan, turn off the heat and allow the fish to cool in the liquid. Otherwise, cover and simmer gently for 5 minutes.

To complete cooking: Remove the cooked fish from saucepan and strain the liquid into a measuring jug. Put the rice into the saucepan, add 500 ml (1 pint) of the liquid and bring to the boil. Stir the rice, cover it, lower the heat and cook gently for 20 minutes. Hard-boil the eggs for 9 minutes, drain and put under cold water for a few minutes, then shell and chop them finely. Melt the butter in a large frying pan and gently fry the onion until golden and soft. Skin and flake the fish, removing any bones, and stir it into the onion, then mix in the oregano, a grating of nutmeg and the chopped eggs. Cover and leave off the heat while the starter is eaten.

To serve: Return to the heat and gently fork the hot rice into the mixture and stir in the crème fraîche. Stir until piping hot. Season to taste with salt and pepper. Sprinkle with the chopped parsley, chives and paprika.

Buttered Crusty Pears

1 brioche loaf
50 g (2 oz) melted butter
4 tablespoons caster or vanilla
    sugar (see p. 186)

4 comice pears
juice of 1 lemon
yogurt or smetana

Can be prepared up to an hour ahead: Cut sufficient slices of brioche about 2 cm (¾ inch thick) to line a wide, shallow ovenproof dish. Dip the slices in the melted butter and lay them in the dish in a single layer. Sprinkle with half the sugar. Peel, quarter, core and slice the pears. Arrange them in overlapping slices all over the top of the pieces of brioche. Sprinkle with lemon juice and the remaining sugar. Cover until ready to cook.

To cook: Heat the oven to Gas 6/400°F/200°C. Bake 20–30 minutes until crusty brown. Can be kept warm in the turned-off oven.

To serve: Serve the yogurt or smetana separately.

Spring Menu 12

Quail eggs with cold meats
Fresh pasta with spring vegetables
Chocolate cream

We begin with a bowl of speckled quail eggs served with a platter of Italian cold meats, *antipasto misto*, and a garnish of green and black olives and gherkins. Buy the best olives you can find, or use ones you yourself have marinated in herbs and spices (see p. 166). The eggs can be boiled a day ahead, or on the day, it's up to you. Arrange the dish just before you eat and serve with olive oil, plenty of bread, and salt and pepper handed separately. Celery salt is particularly good with quail eggs.

Follow the meaty starter with a pasta main course, *pasta primavera*, based on the fresh vegetables and herbs now available in the shops: spring onions, baby courgettes, young new turnips, carrots, mange-tout, French beans and broccoli. The selection can be varied with the seasons and what is available, and could include tomatoes, aubergines, sweet peppers, mushrooms, shelled peas, broad beans or cauliflower. The vegetables are prepared ahead of time, then tossed in oil or butter while the pasta is cooking. Boil the water before you sit down to the starter, then cook the sauce and pasta while everyone else chats over another glass of wine. Parmesan is best bought in a block and grated as and when it is needed.

If your friends are chocolate mousse fans, they will enjoy this dessert. It doesn't use eggs, but simply whipped cream and melted chocolate impregnated with the muscat flavour of elderflowers. It is quite rich, but once tasted no one, not even the most diet conscious, is likely to refuse it. Make it a day or two ahead and serve it with amarettis, Italian macaroons sold in packets or tins, each one individually wrapped in soft tissue paper. A favourite party trick is to light these pieces of paper which waft to the ceiling in spirals of smoke. Failing amarettis, serve ordinary macaroons or almond fingers.

Quail Eggs with Cold Meats

12 quail eggs	green and black olives
450 g (1 lb) selection of	olive oil
Italian cold meats, salami,	sliced Italian or French bread
mortadella, prosciutto etc.	salt
1 jar miniature gherkins	black pepper

Can be done several hours before or day ahead: Boil the eggs for 3 minutes, then drain. To halt the cooking process and prevent a dark ring forming around the yolks, put them into a bowl and stand it under running cold water for several minutes. Crack each egg, return them to the bowl, cover with fresh water and refrigerate until ready to use.

To serve: Drain eggs and put in a bowl in the centre of a large platter. Arrange the meat around and garnish with the gherkins and olives. Serve olive oil, bread, salt and pepper separately.

Fresh Pasta with Spring Vegetables

1 bunch spring onions, sliced
225 g (8 oz) baby courgettes, thinly sliced
100 g (4 oz) young new turnips, thinly sliced
100 g (4 oz) young carrots, chopped
100 g (4 oz) mange-tout, topped and tailed
100 g (4 oz) French beans, topped, tailed and cut in half
225 g (8 oz) broccoli sprigs, sliced lengthwise
150 ml (¼ pint) olive oil or 100 g (4 oz) concentrated butter (see p. 187)

350–450 g (12–16 oz) fresh pasta, such as fettuccine or tagliatelle
2 cloves garlic, chopped
freshly milled black pepper
mixture of finely chopped fresh herbs, such as parsley and basil or fennel and thyme
2 or 3 tablespoons snipped chives
salt
cayenne pepper
50–75 g (2–3 oz) parmesan cheese

Prepare the vegetables half an hour or so ahead.
Just before sitting down to the starter: Put a large pan of water on to the stove to boil.
To cook sauce and pasta: Heat the oil or butter in a wok or large frying pan. Add salt and a dash of oil to the pan of boiling water and boil the pasta for 3–4 minutes. Add the chopped garlic to the hot oil or butter, let it sizzle and add all the vegetables. Toss them over a high heat for 4 to 5 minutes. Meanwhile, drain the pasta and return to the hot pan to keep warm. When the vegetables are piping hot, turn the pasta into a hot serving bowl, season with freshly milled black pepper and pile the vegetables on top. Sprinkle with the herbs and season well with salt and cayenne pepper.
To serve: Mix vegetables and pasta at the table. Hand round the parmesan separately together with a grater, so that everyone can grate as much as they want on to their food.

Chocolate Cream

200 g (7 oz) plain dark
  chocolate
300 ml (½ pint) double cream

1 tablespoon elderflower
  cordial
amarettis or macaroons

Prepare a day or two ahead: Break up and melt chocolate in a low oven or for a few minutes in the microwave. Whip the double cream with the elderflower cordial until it holds its shape, then beat the chocolate into the cream. Spoon into small bowls or glasses and refrigerate.

To serve: Serve amarettis or macaroons separately.

Summer

Summer Menu 1
Chilled cucumber soup
Persian lamb kebabs
Buttered rice
Rose-scented peaches

Summer Menu 2
Mediterranean platter
Chicken with tuna mayonnaise
Red berries in wine

Summer Menu 3
Almond soup with grapes
Salmon in vine leaves
Buttered fennel
Raspberry tart

Summer Menu 4
Mackerel ceviche
Barbecued or grilled quail
Buttered courgettes
Fruit shortcake

Summer Menu 5
Watercress soup with limes
Sea trout with cucumber
Hazelnut meringue cake

Summer Menu 6
Spanish iced tomato soup
Chicken livers with garlic and thyme
Fresh egg tagliatelli
Fruit platter

Summer Menu 7
Melon with honey mint sauce
Fish tartare with aïoli
Summer pudding

Summer Menu 8
Goat's cheese with tomatoes
Spring chicken with bilberries
Italian baked peaches

Summer Menu 9
Aubergine gratin with sweet basil
Trout stuffed with sorrel and watercress
Warm potato salad
Redcurrant meringue cake

Summer Menu 10
Marinated green asparagus tips
Pork chops with pimientoes
Blueberry pie

Summer Menu 11
Melon, pineapple or figs with raw ham
Tuna in a bed of lettuce
Battered cherries

Summer Menu 12
Tomato and peach salad
Chicken and sweet peppers
Steamed new potatoes
Strawberry shortbread

Summer Menu 1

Chilled cucumber soup
Persian lamb kebabs
Buttered rice
Rose-scented peaches

This supper, for which nearly everyhing can be prepared ahead, is inspired by my memories of Tehran in the sixties, where in summer the day-time temperature reached 100° and it was far too hot to eat. So like everyone else we ate at night, cooking under the stars and spicing the air with a smell of woodsmoke, charcoal and grilling meat. The soup, *mast va khiar*, as refreshing as it is pretty with its contrasting colours of creamy yogurt, green cucumber and black raisins, needs time to chill, so make it in the morning or the day before.

The lamb needs to be marinated for up to 3 days, and the longer it is left the more tender it will be. Sumac grows wild in the mountains of Persia and in other parts of the Middle East. The seeds are ground into a red powder which adds a fruity sourness to Middle Eastern dishes. Sumac can be found in some ethnic shops or delicatessens, but if it's unobtainable lemon juice can be used instead. The kebabs can be grilled indoors or barbecued, but the secret is to make sure that the heat source is very hot and to add no oil, which simply causes smoke. Serve the skewered meat garnished with watercress. Buttered rice served with raw egg yolks, which the Persians call *chelo*, is the usual accompaniment but the cooking method is quite complicated, so I have given a simplified version. Offer naan bread as well, plain or spiced.

The meal ends with a delicately scented salad of peaches which can be made an hour or two ahead and kept cool in the fridge. Peel the peaches by first steeping them in boiling water and slice them by cutting vertically towards the stone.

Chilled Cucumber Soup

4 tablespoons raisins
600 ml (1 pint) low-fat yogurt
300 ml (½ pint) single cream
1 cucumber, finely chopped
bunch of spring onions,
　chopped

salt
white pepper
1 tablespoon chopped parsley
1 tablespoon chopped dill or
　fennel

Several hours ahead or night before: Soak the raisins in cold water. Mix the yogurt with the cream in a tureen, and add the chopped cucumber and spring onions. Season to taste with salt and pepper. Drain raisins and mix them in, then cover and refrigerate.

To serve: If the soup seems too thick, add a little cold water. Garnish with the chopped parsley and dill or fennel.

Persian Lamb Kebabs

450–750 g (1–1½ lb) lean
　boned lamb, cut into
　bite-sized cubes
1 onion, grated
2 cloves garlic, chopped
few strands of saffron or
　1 teaspoon powdered
　saffron

freshly milled black pepper
1–2 teaspoons sumac or juice
　of 1 lemon
bunch of watercress
2 lemons, quartered

One to three days ahead: Put the cubed lamb into a china or glass dish with the onion, garlic, saffron, pepper and sumac or lemon juice. Cover and keep in a cool place.

To cook: Thread the meat on to skewers. Prepare the barbecue or heat grill, then grill the kebabs for 5–10 minutes, turning them over once or twice. The kebabs can be kept hot on a warm dish covered in foil in a warm oven while the first course is eaten.

To serve: Serve garnished with the watercress and lemon quarters.

Buttered rice

1 tablespoon oil
1 onion, chopped
250 g (8 oz) basmati or
    long-grained rice
500 ml (1 pint) boiling water

1 teaspoon salt
50 g (2 oz) butter
4 egg yolks, each in a half
    shell

To cook: Heat the oil in a heavy-based saucepan and fry the onion until golden. Stir in the rice and cook over a medium heat for a few minutes. Pour in the boiling water, taking care it does not splutter and burn you. Add salt, cover, lower the heat and cook very gently for 20 minutes. Set aside, covered, for 10 minutes. Stir in the butter and keep warm until ready to eat.
To serve: Put the rice on individual plates, and make a hollow in the centre of each to hold an egg yolk in its half shell. At table, everyone mixes their rice and yolk together.

Rose-scented Peaches

4–6 ripe peaches, peeled and
    sliced
juice of 1 lemon

2–3 tablespoons caster or
    vanilla sugar (see p. 186)
2 tablespoons rosewater

Can be prepared an hour or two ahead: Divide peaches between 4 wine glasses. Sprinkle with lemon juice and sugar. Cover and refrigerate.
To serve: Sprinkle with the rosewater.

Summer Menu 2

Mediterranean platter
Chicken with tuna mayonnaise
Red berries in wine

This cold Mediterranean supper begins with a colourful selection of summer vegetables and fruit arranged on a large platter, together with a dish of sliced salami. There are many different types of salami, some of which are much better than others, so it's worth going to a good delicatessen or cold meat counter and ask to taste it before you buy. Have it cut very thin. Ideally you should remove the skin before serving, but for a kitchen supper, no one really minds doing this themselves. If salami doesn't appeal to you, offer instead either a bowl of pâté, or canned sardines, or some raw or cured ham, or a range of several different sorts of sliced cold meats.

The main Italian dish of cold poached chicken and tuna, *pollo tonnato*, is garnished with a mayonnaise, home-made or bought, sharpened with lemon, anchovies, capers and gherkins. It should be prepared the day before so that the meat can absorb all the different flavours of the sauce. Rather than using a whole chicken, which needs skinning and boning, I find it saves time to use chicken breasts. This dish is quite rich and needs no accompaniment other than a green salad and plenty of Italian or French bread, although you could offer a bowl of new potatoes dusted with snipped chives and chopped parsley or chervil.

The red berries in wine, flavoured with the rose-scent of sweet geranium leaves, should be prepared at least an hour ahead or at any time during the day. The lemon juice helps to bring out the flavour, especially if the fruit is a little unripe. It is the ideal choice for that brief moment when every fruit stall is laden with raspberries, strawberries, loganberries, tayberries and some-times, if you're lucky, small punnets of alpine strawberries. Sweet geranium leaves are at their most potent when the sun has tinged their edges brown; if you don't grow them, use rosewater instead, which should be bought in small amounts as it loses its perfume if stored for long; or flavour the salad with the scent of elderflowers by adding a spoonful or two of elderflower cordial. The berries themselves are such a treat that they really need no accompaniment, though they do go remarkably well with fromage frais or crème fraîche.

Mediterranean Platter

A *selection of the following:*

3 or 4 quartered tomatoes
100 g (4 oz) Greek olives
1 red pepper, finely sliced
1 green pepper, finely sliced
100 g (4 oz) canned chickpeas
100 g (4 oz) grated carrots
1 jar preserved artichoke hearts
4 fresh figs
225 g (8 oz) salami, thinly sliced
salt
freshly milled black pepper
olive oil
Italian or French bread

To serve: Arrange all the ingredients attractively on a large platter and the salami on a dish. Hand round the salt, pepper, olive oil and bread separately.

Chicken with Tuna Mayonnaise

4 free-range or cornfed chicken breasts, skinned
bay leaf
1 small onion, peeled and quartered
8 peppercorns
salt
sprigs of tarragon, parsley and thyme
300 ml ($\frac{1}{2}$ pint) mayonnaise
100 g (4 oz) can tuna fish in oil, drained
3 or 4 anchovy fillets
6 teaspoons capers, rinsed
salt
freshly milled black pepper
juice of 1–2 lemons, plus 1 lemon cut in wedges
4–6 gherkins, sliced
bunch of watercress

Prepare the day before: Lay the chicken breasts in a single layer in a wide pan with the bay leaf, onion, peppercorns, salt and the sprigs of tarragon, parsley and thyme. Just cover with cold water.

sprigs of tarragon, parsley and thyme. Just cover with cold water.
Bring to the boil, lower heat, cover and simmer for 5–10 minutes
until the chicken feels springy when pressed. Remove from the
pan and allow to cool. (Use the stock for something else). If
making your own mayonnaise (see p. 184) prepare it at this point
and set aside in a bowl. Blend the tuna, anchovy fillets and 4
teaspoons of the capers until smooth, then fold into the mayonnaise. Add salt, pepper and lemon juice to taste. Slice the chicken
breasts. Put half the chicken on a serving platter and cover with
half the sauce. Put the remaining chicken on top and spread over
the remaining sauce. Cover and refrigerate until next day.
To serve: Garnish with the sliced gherkins, the remaining
2 teaspoons of capers, lemon wedges and the watercress.

Red Berries in Wine

750 g (1½ lb) selection of 2
  or 3 summer berries
  (raspberries, strawberries,
  tayberries, loganberries,
  alpine strawberries etc)
3–4 tablespoons caster or
  vanilla sugar (see p. 186)
juice of ½ lemon

1 or 2 scented geranium
  leaves or 1 teaspoon
  rosewater
150 ml (¼ pint) dry white
  wine or dry cider
fromage frais or crème fraîche
  (see p. 187)

Prepare one or several hours ahead: Hull the fruits as necessary
and combine them in a bowl with the caster sugar, lemon juice
and scented geranium leaves or rosewater. Cover and put in the
fridge.
To serve: Pour over the wine or cider. Hand round the fromage
frais or crème fraîche separately.

Summer Menu 3

Almond soup with grapes
Salmon in vine leaves
Buttered fennel
Raspberry tart

This supper begins with an elegant cold soup from Andalucia in southern Spain which is made hours ahead or the day before the meal. It is a kind of white *gazpacho* (the word means soaked bread), called *ajo blanco con uvas* and is of Moorish origin. It was adopted by the Spanish long before tomatoes and peppers, which we normally associate with *gazpacho*, arrived from South America. As well as almonds and grapes, it uses garlic, bread, olive oil, and wine vinegar and is very quick to make, especially if you have a food processor. The grapes really do need peeling unless their skins are especially thin, so to speed up the job, put them in a bowl, pour boiling water over them and wait a minute or two. You'll then find it is quite easy. Of course, it is in keeping with the informality of a kitchen supper if you just put them in a bowl and encourage everyone to help themselves and peel their own.

Although the main course is delicious cold, it can be served hot if the weather turns unkind. The steaks in their green wrapping are opened at the table by each guest. If serving cold, hand round a bowl of new potatoes steamed in their skins and a green salad. Eat hot with buttered fennel which gently stews while the fish is cooking. Either way offer basil sauce, made by stirring 2–3 tablespoons bought *pesto* sauce into thick Greek yogurt. Or try the same recipe using whole red mullet, which in France is nicknamed *bécasses de mer*, woodcock of the sea, because like woodcock it is commonly eaten ungutted or with just the livers left in. If you go for these, ask the fishmonger to trim and scale the fish for you, as this is a somewhat tedious job. The vine leaves can be fresh or ones preserved in brine which you find in packets in some supermarkets and ethnic shops. You could also use spinach or lettuce leaves, blanched for 2–3 minutes in boiling, salted water. The dish can be prepared just before it is cooked or several hours ahead.

The raspberry tart needs no cooking if you use a bought, baked pastry shell and it can be assembled in minutes just before the meal. Of course, make your own some days ahead if you'd rather, and store it in an airtight tin. I give no recipe, because I assume that if you are adept at pastry-making and baking blind, you will have your own method. This really simple tart is just as good with other fruit, such as blueberries or perhaps a mixture of tayberries, raspberries and loganberries.

Almond Soup with Grapes

100 g (4 oz) slices stale white bread, crusts removed
100 g (4 oz) ground almonds
3 cloves garlic, peeled and crushed
6 tablespoons olive oil
750 ml (1¼ pint) cold water

salt
2–3 tablespoons white or red wine vinegar
100 g (4 oz) seedless grapes, peeled
handful or two of croûtons (see p. 183)

Prepare at least two hours and up to one day ahead: Soak bread for a minute or two in cold water. Squeeze out as much of the moisture as possible and put into the food processor. Add the almonds and crushed garlic and blend until smooth. Gradually blend in the olive oil in a slow stream, a tablespoon at a time and then blend in half the water. If you haven't got a food processor, use a pestle and mortar. Mash bread, almonds and garlic together before gradually beating in the olive oil and adding water. Turn the soup into a tureen and stir in the remaining water. Add salt and vinegar to taste. Add the peeled grapes and refrigerate.
To serve: Serve with a tablespoon or so of croûtons scattered on top, and put the remainder into a small bowl for everyone to help themselves.

Salmon in Vine Leaves

12 vine leaves   salt
4 salmon steaks   freshly milled black pepper
4 cloves garlic, chopped   juice of 1 lemon
4 sprigs of rosemary   olive oil
4 sprigs of thyme   1 lemon, quartered

Can be prepared several hours ahead: To rid preserved vine leaves of their saltiness, cover them with boiling water, leave for a few minutes, then rinse under the cold tap. Butter a shallow ceramic or glass oven-proof dish. Lay each steak on 3 overlapping leaves. Sprinkle with garlic, lay sprigs of herbs on top, season with salt and pepper, lemon juice and a dash of olive oil. Wrap the leaves round each steak to form parcels and put them close together in the dish. Sprinkle generously with olive oil.

To cook: Heat oven to Gas 5/375°F/190°C and bake for 20–25 minutes. If serving cold, set aside to cool.

To serve: Garnish with lemon quarters and serve from the dish.

Buttered Fennel

750 g (1½ lb) fennel bulbs   salt
50–75 g (2–3 oz) butter   freshly milled black pepper
1 onion, finely chopped

Can be prepared ahead: Wipe bulbs, cut off and discard green stalks and any brown patches, and slice the fennel (save the feathery leaves). Blanch the fennel for 5 minutes in boiling salted water, then drain.

To cook: Melt the butter in a pan, add the onion and the fennel, season with salt and pepper and stew gently for 30 minutes until the fennel is golden brown and tender. Shake the pan from time to time to prevent sticking.

To serve: Chop the feathery leaves and sprinkle over the cooked fennel.

Raspberry Tart

200 ml (7 fl oz) fromage frais
200 ml (7 fl oz) crème fraîche
(see p. 187)
20 cm (8 in) sweet pastry
shell

350 g (12 oz) raspberries
3 tablespoons caster or vanilla
sugar (see p. 186)
1–2 tablespoons toasted,
chopped hazelnuts

Can be prepared an hour or two ahead: Mix fromage frais and crème fraîche and fill the pastry shell. Mix raspberries with the sugar.

To serve: Pile raspberries on to the cream and sprinkle with the hazelnuts.

Summer Menu 4

Mackerel ceviche
Barbecued or grilled quail
Buttered courgettes
Fruit shortcake

We begin with a method of 'cooking' fish in lime or lemon juice which comes from Latin America. I like to think it was invented by the Aztecs, but it is more likely to have originated in Polynesia. There are many variations, including this one for summer mackerel, but you could use any firm-fleshed fish such as salmon, trout, cod, hake, brill, halibut etc. Whatever fish you use, it should be very fresh. Ceviche can be prepared up to 3 days ahead, the finishing touches added just before you eat, but if you want to prepare it on the day, you must do so at least 5 hours before the meal.

Quail – or spring chicken, if you can't get quail – are delicious grilled, and are perfect over a barbecue. They can be put into the marinade several hours ahead. I give them a zip with a sprinkling of mixed black, green, pink and white peppercorns, which are found amongst the spices in kitchen shops, supermarkets and herbalists. Don't add any oil or fat when you barbecue or grill the quail, as this creates all the smoke. One is sufficient per person, but cook more if you want to offer second helpings. Have plenty of French, Italian or naan bread on hand, and either a mixed salad or a dish of buttered courgettes, which can be put on to gently stew just before you sit down at the table. Really small courgettes have a bitter-sweet flavour and are nicest cooked whole. If small ones are not around, use larger ones and cut them diagonally into 2–3 lengths.

Shortcake differs from shortbread in that it uses far less fat in ratio to flour, so the finished dish is more like a crumble, with none of the brittleness of shortbread. Unlike a crumble mix it uses self-raising flour and much less butter. This version uses summer fruits but it can of course be made with other kinds, such as apples or rhubarb. It's nicest eaten warm or cold, served with cream. If you plan to serve it cold, it can be prepared and cooked hours ahead or even the day before; if it is to be eaten warm, assemble it any time on the day and cook just before the meal.

Mackerel Ceviche

350 g (12 oz) mackerel fillets
4–5 limes or lemons
1–2 green chillies, chopped, seeds discarded
225 g (8 oz) tomatoes, cut in chunks
2 tablespoons olive oil

handful chopped marjoram or oregano
salt
cayenne pepper
1 small onion, finely sliced
handful black olives

Prepare at least five hours and up to three days ahead: Cut the fish into bite-sized pieces, discarding all skin and bones, and put into a china or glass serving dish. Add sufficient lime or lemon juice to cover and refrigerate.

To serve: Drain and return the fish to the dish. Mix in the chopped chillies and tomatoes. Moisten with the oil, sprinkle with the marjoram or oregano, season with salt and cayenne and garnish with the onion broken into rings and the olives.

Barbecued or Grilled Quail

4–8 quail
sprigs of rosemary, sage and
    thyme
freshly milled mixed or black
    pepper
½ teaspoon coriander seeds,
    crushed

½ teaspoon whole allspice,
    crushed
juice of ½ lemon
2 lemons, quartered
bunch of watercress

Prepare at least one or several hours ahead: Using kitchen
scissors, slit each quail down the back, spread it out on a board,
skin-side up and flatten it with a rolling pin, pestle or meat
cleaver. Put the quail in a non-metallic dish (metal and lemon
juice have a chemical reaction) and add the herbs, pepper, spices
and the lemon juice. Cover and leave to marinate.
To cook: Prepare the barbecue or heat the grill. Grill the quail
skin-side down first, and turn after 5 minutes. Cook until they are
golden brown and the juices runs clear when pierced with a sharp
knife, about 10 minutes in all. Serve garnished with lemon
wedges and watercress.

Buttered Courgettes

8–12 small courgettes
2 tablespoons water
50 g (2 oz) butter
salt

freshly milled black pepper
lemon juice
handful chopped parsley

To cook: Wash courgettes and put them in a saucepan with the
water and butter. Cover and stew gently until tender but still firm,
about 15 minutes. Remove the lid and raise the heat to reduce the
liquid. Season with salt and pepper and a generous squeeze of
lemon juice, and sprinkle with parsley.

Fruit Shortcake

450 g (1 lb) mixture of 2 or 3 soft fruits, choosing from: raspberries, tayberries, loganberries, strawberries, black or redcurrants, gooseberries and blackberries

2 or 3 tablespoons caster or vanilla sugar (see p. 186)

150 g (6 oz) self-raising flour, or use plain flour with 1 level teaspoon baking powder

75 g (3 oz) soft brown sugar

50 g (2 oz) butter

300 ml (½ pint) single cream

Can be prepared several hours ahead: Prepare the fruit, put into a shallow oven-proof dish and sprinkle over the caster or vanilla sugar. Mix the flour and brown sugar and rub in the butter (or blend in a food processor). Sprinkle over the fruit.

To cook: Heat the oven to Gas 5/375°F/190°C, and bake the pudding for 25–30 minutes. It will keep warm quite happily in the turned-off oven. Hand round the cream separately.

Summer Menu 5

Watercress soup with limes
Sea trout with cucumber
Hazelnut meringue cake

A cold supper for the height of summer begins with a soup that is also good hot should the weather turn chilly. It was introduced to me by my friend Lynda Johnson who made it on the day, and when it was cool, put it in the freezer for an hour or two. You might prefer to make it the day before and chill it in the fridge. The flavour of the limes is unobtrusive but brings out the taste of the other ingredients. If limes are not available, use lemons instead.

Sea trout, which live in the sea but enter the rivers to spawn, are the most succulent of fish with pale-pink, delicate flesh. They are in season from February to September. First cousins to brown trout – which live entirely in fresh water – they are the same family as salmon, and are often sold as salmon trout. Sea trout are best cooked very simply – either poached or baked in foil – and eaten cold. (The same method can be used to cook salmon.) Serve with mayonnaise, either homemade (see p. 184) or a good quality commercial variety jazzed up with a tablespoon or two of bought *pesto* sauce. Otherwise buy a pot of crème fraîche, mix it with a squeeze of lemon juice, a tablespoon or two of horseradish sauce and stir in a handful of chopped walnuts. I would offer only simple accompaniments, perhaps new potatoes either boiled or steamed and a green salad.

The texture of hazelnut meringue cake is quite unlike the brittleness of true meringue, being soft and moist. It can be cooked several days ahead and stored in an air-tight tin. It should be filled 3–4 hours ahead with the whipped cream and fruit, which can be all raspberries or kiwifruit or a mixture of the two. When fresh raspberries are not available, make it with frozen, which should be defrosted and drained. You can buy roasted hazelnuts but otherwise roast your own by putting them under a hot grill, but not too close, until they turn brown. Grind them in a food processor or coffee grinder and store in a screw-top jar. When time is just too pressing, spread cream and fruit over a bought meringue case.

Watercress Soup with Limes

50 g (2 oz) butter
1 onion, chopped
350 g (12 oz) new potatoes, sliced
bunch of watercress, roughly chopped
1 litre (1¾ pints) water
bay leaf
freshly grated nutmeg or pinch powdered

salt
freshly milled black pepper
3 whole limes or 2 lemons
1 lime or ½ lemon, finely sliced
handful chopped chervil or parsley

Prepare several hours ahead or day before: Melt the butter in a saucepan and add the chopped onion, potatoes and watercress, cover and let them sweat for 10 minutes. Add the water, bay leaf, nutmeg, salt, pepper and the grated rind and juice of 2 limes (or 1½ lemons). Simmer, covered, for 20–30 minutes until the potatoes are soft. Put through a blender, liquidizer or mouli-légumes. Cool and refrigerate.

To serve: Serve cold or heated through. Taste and if necessary add more lime or lemon juice. Garnish with the lime or lemon slices and the chopped chervil or parsley.

Sea Trout with Cucumber

1–1.5 kg (2¼–3 lb) sea trout	12 peppercorns
salt	2 tablespoons wine vinegar
sprigs of herbs like parsley,	½–1 cucumber, sliced
fennel, dill, thyme	1–2 lemons, quartered
bay leaf	

Prepare at least five hours ahead: Put the fish into a wide shallow pan or fish kettle and just cover it with water. Add salt, herbs, bay leaf, peppercorns and wine vinegar. Bring slowly to the boil and let it bubble for 2 minutes. Cover and remove from heat. Leave to cool.

(Or bake in foil: Heat the oven to Gas 2/300°F/150°C. Cut a piece of foil large enough to enclose the fish and oil it. Lay the fish on top. Season it with salt and pepper and squeeze over the juice of a lemon. Wrap the foil around the fish in a loose parcel, twisting the ends to prevent cooking juices leaking. Bake 12 minutes for each 450 g (1 lb). Remove from the oven and leave to cool in the foil.)

Carefully lift out the fish and set it on a board or large dish. Peel away the skin, roll fish over and peel other side. Cover with foil until ready to eat.

To serve: Garnish the sea trout with the cucumber slices and lemon quarters.

Hazelnut Meringue Cake

4 egg whites
225 g (8 oz) vanilla sugar
  (see p. 186) or use caster
  sugar and add a few drops
  vanilla essence to the
  whipped whites
½ teaspoon white wine vinegar

100 g (4 oz) ground, roasted
  hazelnuts
300 ml (½ pint) double cream,
  whipped
225 g (8 oz) raspberries or 4
  kiwifruit peeled and sliced
  or a mixture of the two

Prepare one to several days ahead: Heat the oven to Gas 5/375°F/190°C. Grease 2 × 20 cm (8 in) sandwich tins and line the bases with greaseproof paper. Beat egg whites until stiff and then beat in the sugar, a tablespoon at a time (and the vanilla essence if using caster sugar) and the vinegar. Fold in the hazelnuts. Divide the mixture between the two tins, smoothing it flat, and bake for 30–35 minutes. Turn out on to a wire rack while still warm and peel off the paper. When cold, store in a tin.

Three to four hours ahead: Sandwich the 2 meringue halves together with two-thirds of the cream and fruit. Spread the remaining cream over the top and decorate with the remaining fruit.

Summer Menu 6

Spanish iced tomato soup
Chicken livers with garlic and thyme
Fresh egg tagliatelli
Fruit platter

Although this iced tomato soup, the Spanish *gazpacho*, can be made within 2 hours of the supper, it is best made a day ahead so that it can absorb all the flavours. It takes only minutes to make using a food processor or liquidizer. Traditionally, this peasant soup is thickened with bread to provide a filling midday meal: this version is lighter and makes a refreshing summer starter. It is served here with black olives and croûtons and can be accompanied by small bowls of chopped tomato, cucumber and hard-boiled egg, but the soup is good even without these adornments, and if the weather suddenly turns chilly, it can be served hot.

The chicken livers require a certain amount of showmanship because they are cooked in front of the guests and flamed at the table. Watch out in your zeal not to flame the table too! In this country chicken livers are nearly always sold frozen, and it's important to make sure they are thoroughly defrosted and drained. If you have no brandy, you can use whisky, calvados, gin or vodka, or whatever spirit you might have on hand. Serve the livers with a simple green salad, fresh egg tagliatelli mixed with *pesto* sauce and a basketful of French or Italian bread.

The dessert has the same visual impact as a platter of vegetable *crudités*. A selection of raw fruit is arranged attractively on a flat dish. Everyone helps themselves, dipping the fruit if they wish into a bowl of fromage frais or crème fraîche. Be generous with the paper napkins. All sorts of summer fruits can be used: sliced peaches and nectarines, plums and greengages, black and green grapes. The secret is to contrast colours and textures. In the selection below green-fleshed kiwifruit, yellow-skinned galia melon, and strawberries are grouped with figs and paper-dry physalis (Chinese lanterns) with their orange berry centres. Assemble it just before the meal.

Spanish Iced Tomato Soup

1 onion, roughly chopped
1 cucumber, roughly chopped
1 green pepper, roughly chopped
2 cloves garlic, chopped or crushed
2 tablespoons wine vinegar
2 tablespoons olive oil
1 can Italian chopped tomatoes
450 ml (¾ pint) tomato juice
salt
freshly milled black pepper
100 g (4 oz) black olives
100 g (4 oz) croûtons (see p. 183)

Prepare at least two hours and up to one day ahead: Put roughly chopped onion, cucumber, green pepper and garlic into a blender, switch on and add vinegar and oil. When blended, add the chopped tomatoes and tomato juice. Put into a tureen and mix well. Alternatively, chop vegetables small and pound them in a mortar, gradually stirring in the vinegar and oil before mixing with the chopped tomatoes and tomato juice in the tureen. Season to taste with salt and pepper and refrigerate.

To serve: Serve the soup from the tureen and hand the olives and croûtons for everyone to help themselves.

Chicken Livers with Garlic and Thyme

2 tablespoons flour
salt
freshly milled black pepper
450 g (1 lb) chicken livers
2 tablespoons olive oil

25 g (1 oz) butter
2 cloves garlic, chopped
sprigs of fresh thyme or
   1 teaspoon dried
2 tablespoons brandy

Can be done ahead: Put the flour into a paper or plastic bag and season with salt and pepper.

To cook: Put the livers into the bag with the flour and shake until they are well coated. Heat the oil in a frying pan and when it is hot float the butter in it. Let it melt, then fry the livers over a medium heat, letting them brown slightly before turning them over. Add the garlic and thyme. Toss the livers to mix well with the herbs. Heat the brandy in a metal ladle or small saucepan. Bring the pan to the table, light the brandy and pour it flaming over the livers. Serve when the flames die down.

Fresh Egg Tagliatelli

225 g (8 oz) fresh egg
   tagliatelli
salt

oil
1 jar of *pesto* sauce

To cook: Bring a large pan of salted water to the boil. Add a dash of oil and boil the pasta for 3 minutes. Drain well, put into a bowl and stir in the *pesto*.

Fruit Platter

selection of summer fruits
 such as the following:
2 kiwifruit, skinned and
 thinly sliced
225 g (8 oz) strawberries,
 unhulled
1 small ripe galia melon,
 deseeded and sliced thinly

8–12 physalis (Chinese
 lanterns)
4–8 figs

bowl of fromage frais,
 mascarpone or crème
 fraîche (see p. 187)
bowl of caster sugar

Prepare just before the meal: Arrange the fruit on a platter. Serve the fromage frais, mascarpone or crème fraîche and sugar separately.

Summer Menu 7

Melon with honey mint sauce
Fish tartare with aïoli
Summer pudding

In the middle of a heatwave, this is an attractive supper involving little cooking. It begins quite simply with melon served with a tangy mint sauce. To choose a ripe melon, press the stem end, which should yield a little. Charentais, ogen, galia, canteloupe and Persian melons have a sweet, heady perfume and bright flesh varying from orange, to yellow and green. Honeydews, though cheaper, tend to lack flavour. Make the honey mint sauce any time during the day or the evening before, as it needs time to cool. Cut and deseed the melon and sprinkle it with lemon juice an hour or so ahead.

The fish, which is eaten raw, must be very fresh so only buy it from a fishmonger you can trust, and tell him the reason why the fish must be in prime condition. Use tuna, salmon, or freshwater or sea trout. The finely chopped fish is marinated with flavourings and lemon juice – which acts as a cooking agent – for at least 2 hours before it is eaten, so that it absorbs the taste of shallots, gherkins, capers and herbs. It is worth setting aside the time to make your own aïoli but if you really can't or don't want to do this, crush the garlic and stir it into a good quality bought mayonnaise. This is a rich and filling dish which is eaten on its own with plenty of crusty bread.

Summer Pudding, that most traditional of English puddings, can be made up to 3 days ahead. When you're in a particular hurry it's quickest with just raspberries, which need no preparation. When you have a bit more time add redcurrants and/or blackcurrants which must be stripped from their stems. It's easiest to do this with the prongs of a fork and the result is worth the extra effort. The pudding should be set aside for at least a day for the bread to absorb the concentrated flavour and deep red juice of the fruits.

Melon with Honey Mint Sauce

4 tablespoons dry cider or white wine
1 tablespoon honey
1 teaspoon cider vinegar

3 tablespoons chopped fresh mint
2 small ripe melons or 1 large
juice of 1 lemon

Prepare several hours or day ahead: Put cider, honey and vinegar into a saucepan and heat gently, stirring until the honey dissolves. Cool and mix with the mint.

Prepare an hour or so ahead: Cut small melons in half – large into quarters – and remove the seeds. If using small melons, you may need to cut a small sliver off each base so that they can stand upright. Put on to plates and sprinkle with lemon juice.

To serve: Pour the sauce into the hollows of the small melons, or serve it separately if using melon quarters.

Fish Tartare with *Aïoli*

450–750 g (1–1½ lb) fresh tuna, salmon, trout or sea trout

salt
freshly milled black pepper
juice of 3 lemons

3 shallots or spring onions,
  finely chopped
5 or 6 large gherkins,
  chopped
1 tablespoon capers
handful chopped chervil,
  fennel, dill or coriander
  leaves, plus 4 sprigs
watercress to garnish

4 tomatoes, quartered

for the aïoli:
4 cloves garlic, crushed
2 egg yolks
300 ml (½ pint) olive oil
salt
freshly milled black pepper

Prepare at least two hours ahead: Chop the fish finely, discarding all skin and bones. Season with salt and pepper and gently mix with the lemon juice, shallots or onion, gherkins, capers and the chopped herbs. Put into a dish, cover and refrigerate for at least 2 hours. Make the *aïoli* by crushing the garlic in a mortar with a pestle (or use a food processor). Beat in the egg yolks. Add the oil drop by drop at first as for a mayonnaise. Beat in sufficient to make a thick sauce, season with salt and pepper to taste and turn into a bowl. Cover and leave in a cool place.

To serve: Put a mound of the fish mixture on each of 4 plates and flatten it slightly. Garnish with the watercress, quartered tomatoes and a sprig of either chervil, fennel, dill or coriander. Hand the *aïoli* separately.

Summer Pudding

450 g (1 lb) raspberries, or a
  mixture of raspberries,
  red- and blackcurrants
100 g (4 oz) caster or vanilla
  sugar (see p. 186)

5 mm (¼ in) slices one-day-old
  white bread, crusts
  removed
300 ml (½ pint) single cream

Prepare one to three days ahead of time: If using currants, strip them from their stalks with a fork and put all the fruit into a saucepan with the sugar. Bring slowly to the boil, stirring occasionally to mix. When the sugar has dissolved simmer for 2– 3 minutes, until the fruit yields its juices. Line a 600 ml (1 pint) pudding basin or soufflé dish with the bread slices, plugging any

gaps with small pieces of bread. Pour in the fruit and juices. Top
with more sliced bread, trimming it to fit. Cover with a flat-
bottomed plate or saucer and weight this down with something
heavy (a flat-iron or a couple of tins perhaps). Refrigerate
overnight – or for 2 to 3 days – until ready to eat.

To serve: Run a knife round the edge and invert on to a serving
dish with a lip to catch the juices. Serve the cream separately.

Summer Menu 8

Goat's cheese with tomatoes
Spring chicken with bilberries
Italian baked peaches

Plan this supper for out-of-doors eating or for the end of summer,
when the temperature begins to drop and the warmth of the oven
becomes an advantage. The starter is based on a salad served by
every Italian restaurant although they use mozzarella cheese. Too
often the kind we buy is uninteresting and rubbery, so I use goat's
cheese marinated to a French recipe and the result is much more
exciting. The cheese must be put into the marinade at least a day
before it is to be eaten and is even better after a week. The salad
itself takes only minutes to prepare. Preserved lemon peel adds its
own special flavour and can be bought in jars, or it's easy enough
to make your own (see p. 185), but in any case it is an optional
extra.

  Spring chicken can be bland, but cooked in this way, which is
based on a Breton recipe originally for quail, they acquire an
almost gamey flavour. If you can't get hold of bilberries, use their
more easily obtainable cousin, the blueberry. One spring chicken
can feed two, but I've allowed for healthy appetites and specified
one each. The birds take only minutes to prepare and are then
simmered gently for 45 minutes. They can be kept hot, covered in
foil while the starter is eaten. I'm suggesting you serve them with
steamed new potatoes (see p. 80) and watercress, but you could if

you prefer skip the potatoes and offer plenty of French, Italian or wholemeal bread.

Not-quite-ripe summer fruits too often seem to be our lot. One way of dealing with them is to marinate them for an hour or two (slicing larger fruits and leaving smaller ones like strawberries whole) in lemon juice or a light vinegar such as raspberry or more extravagantly balsamic: the acid softens and brings out the flavour of the fruit. Another way of turning slightly hard peaches into a mouthwatering dessert is to cook them by this Italian method. Prepare them at any time during the day and put them into the oven just before you begin the meal. They emerge bathed in pink juice and deliciously flavoured with almond. Serve with crème fraîche, double cream, yogurt or fromage frais.

Goat's Cheese with Tomatoes

2 × 100 g (4 oz) cylindrical
  goat cheeses

for the marinade:
  2 or 3 sprigs thyme and
  rosemary
  1 bay leaf
  1 small red chilli
  1 clove garlic, chopped
  8 peppercorns
  olive oil to cover

450 g (1 lb) ripe tomatoes,
  chopped
1 tablespoon brandy or wine
  vinegar
salt
freshly milled black pepper
handful chopped basil or
  oregano
peel of half a preserved lemon
  cut in strips, optional
  (see p. 185)

Prepare 24 hours or up to a week ahead: Cut each cheese into 3 rounds. Put them in a deepish jar with the herbs, spices and olive oil. Cover and leave to marinate.

Prepare just before the meal: Put the chopped tomatoes into a shallow serving bowl. Quarter the cheese rounds and add to the bowl. Sprinkle over the brandy, or wine vinegar, and 3 or 4 tablespoons of the oil in which the cheese was soaked. Season with salt and pepper and sprinkle with the basil or oregano. Garnish with strips of preserved lemon peel if using.

Spring Chicken with Bilberries

225 g (8 oz) bilberries or
  blueberries
4 spring chickens
8 rashers streaky bacon
2 tablespoons olive oil
2 tablespoons brandy or
  calvados
150 ml (¼ pint) dry cider

sprigs of thyme, parsley and
  chervil
salt
freshly milled black pepper
2 tablespoons wild rowan or
  redcurrant jelly
bunch of watercress

To cook: Put 3–4 bilberries or blueberries inside each chicken; wrap each bird in 2 rashers of bacon and secure with string. Heat the oil in a heavy-based casserole large enough to hold the 4 birds comfortably. Brown them all over. Heat the brandy or calvados in a ladle or small saucepan, light it and pour it flaming over the birds. When the flames die down, pour in the cider and add the herbs, salt and pepper and remaining bilberries or blueberries. Cover and simmer for 1 hour.

To serve: Put the birds on a hot serving dish surrounded by the bilberries or blueberries and cover with foil. Boil the sauce hard until it reduces by half, stir in the wild rowan or redcurrant jelly and pour over the birds. Garnish with the watercress.

Italian Baked Peaches

4–6 peaches
juice of half a lemon
2–3 tablespoons caster or
  vanilla sugar (see p. 186)

50 g (2 oz) macaroons
25 g (1 oz) butter

Can be prepared ahead of time: Butter a shallow oven-proof dish, large enough to hold the halved peaches in one layer. Wash but don't peel them. Slit them in half round their stem end. Ease the 2 halves apart, leaving or removing stones, as you wish. Lay the halves skin-side down in the dish. Sprinkle with lemon juice and sugar. Crumble the macaroons and sprinkle the crumbs over the peaches. Dot with the butter. Cover until ready to cook.

To cook: Heat the oven to Gas 5/375°F/190°C and bake for 20–25 minutes. If you are not ready to eat them, they will remain warm quite happily in the switched-off oven.
To serve: Serve the cream separately.

Summer Menu 9

Aubergine gratin with sweet basil
Trout stuffed with sorrel
and watercress
Warm potato salad
Redcurrant meringue cake

Aubergines, courgettes and tomatoes flavoured with the heady scent of sweet basil combine to make this melting and visually attractive southern French dish, *gratin languedocien*. If the weather is warm, plan to eat it and the trout cold, and bake them together the day before. However, if it turns cool, bake them on the evening itself as they are just as delicious hot. Sweet basil in pots is widely available in many supermarkets or good green-grocers. It is at its best when the leaves are young and fresh, so treat it as you would a bunch of parsley, using it up fairly quickly and buying more when you need it.

Sorrel adds its distinctive bitter-sweet flavour to a simple dish of baked trout. It's an easy plant to grow, coming up year after year, but if you haven't a supply, use spinach instead. The trout can be stuffed just prior to cooking or prepared earlier in the day. Serve them with a warm potato salad which is prepared just before the guests arrive and kept warm until ready to eat. If you make this salad with new potatoes there is no need to peel them, but older potatoes are nicer peeled. This is easiest done once they are cooked, as the skin comes away paper-thin. Choose even-sized potatoes. Warm potato salad need not be confined just to summer: it's good in the winter months too, served as a starter with a platter of cold meats.

End this supper of unpretentious French dishes with a somewhat flamboyant Austrian redcurrant meringue cake, *Ribisel-kuchen*, which juggles the sharpness of the fruit with the musky flavour of almonds and sweet meringue. You could use other summer fruits too such as blueberries or bilberries, or raspberries either on their own or mixed with blackberries, or perhaps a mixture of red-, black- and whitecurrants – whatever is available and best. This pudding is prepared in 2 stages. This is not alarming: each is easy and the final result is worth any effort. The almond cake base can be baked 2 or 3 days ahead. The fruit and meringue topping are added on the day, and the cake goes into a hot oven until golden brown. This can be done well ahead of the supper as it is best eaten warm or cold. Of course, you could always cheat a little by using a bought sponge flan base: cover it with the fruit, sprinkle over a handful of slivered almonds and top with the beaten egg whites and sugar, then bake as in the recipe.

Aubergine Gratin with Sweet Basil

450 g (1 lb) aubergines, peeled and sliced
salt
150 ml (¼ pint) olive or groundnut oil
225 g (8 oz) courgettes, sliced
450 g (1 lb) ripe tomatoes, sliced or 1 can Italian chopped tomatoes

handful sweet basil, chopped
freshly milled black pepper
1 clove garlic, chopped
2–3 tablespoons breadcrumbs (see p. 183)
French or Italian bread

If to be eaten cold, prepare the day before: Put the aubergine slices in a colander, sprinkle them with salt and leave for half an hour. After this time, wipe with kitchen paper. Heat oven to Gas 5/375°F/190°C. Heat half the oil in a flameproof gratin dish and fry the aubergine slices, a few at a time, until they soften. Transfer them to a plate, interleaving each layer with kitchen paper. Add more oil as necessary. Add the courgettes to the pan and fry, turning them over, until golden. Layer courgettes, aubergines and tomatoes in the dish, seasoning each layer with sweet basil, salt and pepper, finishing with a layer of tomatoes. Sprinkle over the garlic, breadcrumbs and more sweet basil and moisten with remaining oil. Bake for 30–40 minutes.

To serve: Serve hot or cold with plenty of French or Italian bread.

Trout Stuffed with Sorrel and Watercress

handful sorrel (or spinach) leaves	4 trout
	salt
bunch watercress	pepper
bunch chives, snipped	150 ml ($\frac{1}{4}$ pint) dry white
2 or 3 sprigs of mint, chopped	wine

Can be prepared several hours ahead: Put sorrel and watercress into a saucepan over a medium heat and reduce until soft, 2–3 minutes. Drain well and leave to cool.

To cook: Heat the oven to Gas 5/375°F/190°C. Mix snipped chives and mint with the sorrel and watercress and fill the cavities of the fish with this mixture. Lay them in an oiled oven dish, season with salt and pepper and pour over the wine. Bake for 25–30 minutes, basting half-way through the cooking time.

Warm Potato Salad

900 g (2 lb) new potatoes	salt
2 cloves garlic, chopped	freshly milled black pepper
2 tablespoons wine vinegar	handful chopped parsley or
4 tablespoons olive oil	chervil

To cook: Bring a pan of salted water to the boil, add potatoes and simmer for 20 minutes until soft but still firm. Drain and slice into a bowl. Sprinkle with the garlic, vinegar, olive oil, salt and pepper and mix gently. Garnish with the chopped parsley or chervil and serve warm.

Redcurrant Meringue Cake

150 g (6 oz) flour
50 g (2 oz) ground almonds
50 g (9 oz) caster or vanilla
  sugar (see p. 186)

75 g (3 oz) butter
3 eggs
225 g (8 oz) redcurrants

Base can be prepared one to three days ahead: Heat the oven to Gas 4/350°F/180°C. Mix flour, ground almonds and 75 g (3 oz) sugar in the bowl of a food processor. Add the butter, cut in pieces, and process until you have fine crumbs. Separate eggs and blend in the yolks one at a time, reserving the whites. Process until the mixture holds together, although it will be fairly crumbly. Empty it into a 24 cm (9 in) flan tin with a removable base and press it down with your fingers until it covers the base evenly. Smooth with the back of a spoon. Bake for 25 minutes. Cool and keep in a tin until ready to use. Keep the egg whites in the fridge, covered.

To cook cake: Heat the oven to Gas 7/425°F/220°C. Remove stalks from redcurrants by stripping them with the prongs of a fork. Lay them on the pastry base and sprinkle with 75 g (3 oz) of the sugar, leaving a margin all round. Whip egg whites until stiff and beat in remaining 75 g (3 oz) of sugar. Cover the top completely with the meringue. Bake for 15–20 minutes until the top is golden brown.

To serve: Serve warm or cold.

Summer Menu 10

Marinated green asparagus tips
Pork chops with pimientos
Blueberry pie

This simple Spanish starter, *trigueros en vinagrillo*, is not cheap but the simplicity and speed of preparation compensates for the cost. It calls for asparagus tips, which supermarkets often sell during the summer months. Prepare them at least 2 hours ahead, longer if you wish, so that they can absorb the spices. Serve with crusty bread to mop up the sauce.

The Spanish mood continues with *chilindrón*, moist and tender pork chops in a melting sauce of *pimientos*, tomatoes and onions. The sweet peppers should be baked and skinned but to save time I suggest using either preserved sliced peppers, *peperoni* or Spanish canned red *pimientos*. Serve the chops with steamed new potatoes (see p. 80), dusted with chopped basil. If you are eating out of doors, you could cook the chops just before the meal and keep them warm covered in foil in the oven while the first course is eaten.

Blueberry pie is perhaps the most famous of American desserts. The fruit, first cousin to wild bilberries, is now being cultivated in this country. The berries turn from blue to crimson when cooked and give out a lot of juice, so there are two things to do to prevent a soggy pie: the first is to coat them in flour, which thickens the sauce; the second is not to add sugar until just before baking, as sugar makes the juices run. To save time I'm suggesting puff-pastry sheets but if you prefer use a block of either puff or shortcrust pastry and roll it out to fit your dish. Blueberry pie is eaten warm or cold, but if using puff pastry bake it on the day it is to be eaten, as it goes limp if baked the day before. This problem does not arise if you use short-crust pastry.

Marinated Green Asparagus Tips

450 g (1 lb) green asparagus tips
8 tablespoons olive oil
2 tablespoons red wine vinegar
4 cloves garlic, crushed
1 teaspoon paprika
2 tablespoons of the cooking liquid
salt
freshly milled black pepper

Prepare at least two hours ahead: Put asparagus into a shallow pan, barely cover with water and simmer, covered, until tender, 5–10 minutes. Drain. Put 2 tablespoons of the liquid into a screwtop jar with the remaining ingredients and shake to mix.

Arrange the asparagus in a shallow dish, pour over the dressing and leave to marinate for at least 2 hours.

Pork Chops with *Pimientos*

2 tablespoons olive oil
4 lean pork chops or
  escalopes
1 onion, chopped
1 clove garlic, chopped or
  crushed

½ jar *peperoni* or 1 can
  pimientos, sliced
1 can Italian chopped
  tomatoes, drained
salt
freshly milled black pepper

To cook: Heat the oil in a wide flame-proof casserole and brown the chops all over, in 2 batches if necessary. Take out the chops and fry the onion until golden brown, add garlic and cook a minute or two before stirring in the *peperoni* or *pimientos* and drained tomatoes. Return the chops, season with salt and pepper, cover and simmer for 20 minutes until the meat is cooked. Test by piercing with a skewer; the juices should run clear, not pink.
To serve: Put the chops on a warm serving dish. Boil the sauce hard for a few minutes, stirring at intervals, until it reduces to a jammy consistency. Pour the sauce round the chops: they can be kept warm covered in foil in the oven.

Blueberry Pie

2 sheets ready-rolled puff
  pastry or 225 g (8 oz) puff
  or shortcrust cut in half
  and rolled out
225 g (8 oz) blueberries
1 tablespoon flour

4 tablespoons caster or vanilla
  sugar (see p. 186)
½ teaspoon cinnamon or
  nutmeg
25 g (1 oz) butter
cream, fromage frais or
  yogurt

Can be done ahead: Line an 18 cm (7 in) sandwich tin with 1 sheet of pastry. Wash the berries and put the flour into a bag. Add the berries and shake well so that each one is coated. Put them on top of the pastry, sprinkle over the cinnamon or nutmeg and dot with the butter.

To cook: Heat the oven to Gas 6/400°F/200°C. Sprinkle 3 tablespoons sugar over the fruit. Dampen the edges of the pastry, lay the second sheet on top, fold the edges of the lower sheet over the upper one and seal carefully. Slash the top 2 or 3 times for the steam to escape and brush with water. Sprinkle over the remaining tablespoon of sugar. Bake for 30–35 minutes, until the pastry is golden.

To serve: Allow to cool. Serve warm or cold with cream, fromage frais or yogurt handed round separately.

 ## Summer Menu 11

Melon, pineapple or figs
with raw ham
Tuna in a bed of lettuce
Battered cherries

In summer, if you have a balcony, patio or garden, not every meal need be confined to the kitchen. Nothing is nicer than setting a table out of doors and this supper, with its hot main course and warm dessert, is ideal for such an occasion. If this is not possible, save this menu for one of those cool evenings at the end of the season. It begins with a cold starter of fruit with raw ham. It's important to use one of the hams which are specially cured for eating uncooked, like Parma which is the most famous and rather expensive. There are however cheaper and delicious alternatives like France's Bayonne or those sold under the generic name of *prosciutto*. Melon or figs and ham is something of a cliché in Italian restaurants, but this combination is discovered all over southern Europe and in Spain raw ham with pineapple is also eaten. It is a dish which is simple to prepare either just before you eat, or an hour or two ahead. These fruits also go well with other kinds of cold meat, for example a selection of sliced, cured sausages such as mortadella, salami, and garlic sausage, or perhaps smoked chicken. Offer plenty of crusty bread as well and a bowl of unsalted butter. Melon and pineapple are nicest cold, but figs benefit from being left to gently warm in the sun for an hour or two.

The main course, which uses fresh tuna, is based on a Provençal recipe, *thon à la chartreuse*. The fish can be laid in its bed of onions, tomatoes and lettuce leaves hours before it goes into the oven, or just before, but remember to allow sufficient time for it to cook, 1½ hours. I like to use fleshy, round Provençal tomatoes which are full of flavour, and less watery than our northern varieties. Some are now being imported, although as they are shipped unripe, they never really develop the flavour of those which redden in the sun. When these are unavailable, I use that familiar stalwart, a can of Italian chopped tomatoes, well drained. Tuna is meaty and filling, and this dish needs no other accompaniment than perhaps steamed or boiled new potatoes, or just a lot of crisp, fresh French or Italian bread.

The cherry pudding, which is made with a rich batter rather like our Yorkshire pudding, is in fact a French *clafoutis* which appears in various guises all over France; this is the famous version from the Limousin. Other regions use other fruits, grapes, apples or pears, plums or prunes or a mixture of any of these. The pudding can be assembled hours ahead and is then baked for 45–50 minutes. It is nicest warm or cold, rather than piping hot from the oven. This recipe works well with canned, pitted black cherries but if you want to use fresh, buy a cherry or olive stoner and it will take only minutes to stone them. If you balk at this, leave the stones in and explain that these give the finished pudding its almondy flavour! Only the most pompous will object to the opportunity to play 'tinker, tailor,' at the end of the meal.

Melon, Pineapple or Figs with Raw Ham

8–12 ripe figs, washed or
  1 ogen, charentais or galina
  melon thinly sliced,
  de-seeded and peeled or
  1 pineapple, cut in rings

lemon juice
freshly milled black pepper
8 slices prosciutto

To serve: Arrange the figs in a bowl and the ham on a flat platter; *or* sprinkle the melon or pineapple slices with lemon juice and pepper and arrange them on a wide platter with the ham.

Tuna in a Bed of Lettuce

200 ml (7 fl oz) olive oil
1 cos lettuce
2 onions, sliced
2 cloves garlic, chopped
1 can Italian chopped
    tomatoes, drained, or
    450 g (1 lb) Provençal
    tomatoes, sliced

1 lemon, sliced
salt
freshly milled black pepper
750 g (1½ lb) tuna, in one
    piece
2 tablespoons brandy

Can be prepared several hours ahead: Lightly oil a wide oven-proof dish, line it with lettuce leaves, half the onion, garlic, tomato and lemon slices and season with salt and pepper. Lay the tuna on top, sprinkle with half the olive oil, cover with the remaining lemon, tomato, garlic and onion slices and season again. Cover with several layers of lettuce leaves. Pour over the remaining oil and sprinkle with the brandy.

To cook: Heat the oven to Gas 4/350°F/180°C and bake, uncovered, for 1½ hours.

To serve: Remove the charred leaves on top before bringing to the table.

Battered Cherries

1 can pitted black cherries,
    drained, or 450 g (1 lb)
    cherries, stoned
2 level tablespoons plain flour
2 level tablespoons caster or
    vanilla sugar (see p. 186)
2 eggs

300 ml (½ pint) milk
1 tablespoon oil
1 tablespoon rum, or a fruit
    liqueur such as pear or
    kirsch
2 or 3 tablespoons icing sugar

Can be prepared hours ahead: Butter a shallow oven-proof dish and put the cherries in it. Mix the flour and sugar in a bowl or food processor. Beat in the eggs one at a time, followed by the milk, oil and rum or liqueur. Set aside.

To cook: Heat the oven to Gas 4/350°F/180°C. Beat the batter again and pour over the cherries. Bake for 45–50 minutes, until the filling is set and the top is nicely brown.

To serve: Dust with the icing sugar and serve warm or cold.

Summer Menu 12

Tomato and peach salad
Chicken and sweet peppers
Steamed new potatoes
Strawberry shortbread

Sliced tomatoes and peaches combine in this pretty Italian salad, which may seem a mite bizarre, but is refreshingly different with its added flavours of lemon, sweet basil and walnut oil. It takes just minutes to prepare, and can be made either just before the meal or an hour or so before. Unless the skin is very tough, there's no need to peel the tomatoes or peaches. If you feel you must do so, remember the easy trick of steeping either fruit in boiling water for a few minutes before peeling them.

The chicken and sweet pepper dish is a variation on the theme of that famous Provençal recipe *poulet aux quarante gousses d'ail*, chicken with 40 cloves of garlic, which proved to be one of the most popular recipes in my book *Simple French Cuisine from Provence and Languedoc*. In this case, the whole bird is cooked in a sealed pot with onions, herbs, garlic and sweet peppers. It is a good choice for eating out of doors, or for an evening when the weather turns foul and the oven warmth of the kitchen becomes welcoming. The dish looks most attractive if you combine green, red and yellow peppers. It can be put together just before it goes into the oven, or at any convenient moment during the day. The sealed pot is brought to the table so that everyone can inhale the garlicky aroma as the lid is lifted. I suggest you offer steamed new potatoes which, if you have a hitch in your timetable, are good-natured enough not to spoil if cooked rather longer than the specified cooking time. However, the dish is just as good with rice or small pasta.

Prepare the very English strawberry dessert, which looks luxurious but is surprisingly economical and easy, a day ahead if you like or on the day, but you must allow time for the shortbread to absorb the filling. You could use other soft fruits such as raspberries, chopped peaches or nectarines, bilberries or redcurrants. The chore of making your own shortbread is avoided by using the rounds of petticoat tails which are sold in packets (usually containing 2 rounds) in most supermarkets. This commercially produced shortbread is quite sweet, so the recipe contains no extra sugar.

Tomato and Peach Salad

4–6 ripe tomatoes, sliced
2–3 ripe peaches, sliced
freshly milled black pepper
juice of 1 lemon
salt
3–4 tablespoons walnut oil
handful of basil, chopped

Can be prepared an hour or so ahead: Arrange the sliced tomatoes and peaches on a platter or individual plates. Season with pepper and sprinkle with lemon juice.
To serve: Season with salt and sprinkle with walnut oil and basil.

Chicken and Sweet Peppers

1 cornfed chicken weighing
    about 1.5 kg (3 lb)
salt
freshly milled black pepper
several sprigs of fresh
    rosemary
2 onions, chopped
3 or 4 sweet peppers,
    chopped
8 whole, unpeeled cloves
    garlic
sprig of sage
150 ml (¼ pint) olive oil
1 tablespoon flour

Can be prepared several hours ahead: Use a lidded, earthenware casserole in which the chicken and vegetables will fit comfortably. Season the cavity of the bird with salt and pepper and insert a sprig of rosemary. Put half the chopped onion and peppers into the casserole. Add the whole garlic cloves, sprigs of rosemary and sage. Lay the bird on top, add the remaining onions and peppers and pour over the oil. Mix the flour with sufficient water to make a thick paste. With your finger, wipe a thin strip of the paste all round the rim of the lid, then press the lid into place. Put in a cool place.

To cook: Heat the oven to Gas 5/375°F/190°C and cook the chicken for 1½ hours.

To serve: Bring the casserole to the table, insert a knife under the flour seal and remove the lid to release the mouthwatering aroma.

Steamed New Potatoes

900 g (2 lb) new, even-sized   25 g (1 oz) butter
  potatoes   handful parsley or sweet basil,
salt   chopped
sprig of mint

Put washed but unpeeled potatoes into a steamer over simmering water with a little salt and the sprig of mint. Steam for 25–30 minutes. (If not ready to eat, keep hot over very low heat.) Remove steamer and pour off the water. Melt butter in the saucepan, return the potatoes, shake the pan well until they are coated all over and sprinkle with the parsley or sweet basil.

Strawberry Shortbread

4 rounds shortbread petticoat   225 g (8 oz) strawberries,
  tails   hulled and quartered
300 ml (½ pint) double cream,   1 tablespoon brandy, optional
  whipped

Prepare several hours or one day ahead: Sandwich the rounds of shortbread with three-quarters of the whipped cream and strawberries. Spread remaining cream on top and decorate with strawberries.

To serve: Sprinkle with the brandy.

Autumn

Autumn Menu 1
Mushrooms stuffed with snails or mussels
Rabbit with prunes
Potatoes with celeriac
Black grapes white cheese

Autumn Menu 2
Artichoke hearts with tomatoes
Tunisian lamb with dried fruit
Black and white rice
Honey-glazed pears

Autumn Menu 3
Baby corn with garlic butter
Steak tartare
Potato galette
Pumpkin pie

Autumn Menu 4
Sardines with Italian toast
Pheasant with mushrooms
Garlic fanned potatoes
Upside-down apple tart

Autumn Menu 5
Prawns with mushrooms and anchovies
Moroccan baked grey mullet
Fruit pancakes

Autumn Menu 6
Pear and walnut salad
Toulouse sausages with garlic
Italian coffee cheese

Autumn Menu 7
Mussels in cider
Mushrooms with bacon and pasta
Watercress and orange salad
Blackberry autumn pudding

Autumn Menu 8
Chestnut soup
Venison with olives
Chicory and orange salad
Apricot fool

Autumn Menu 9
Olive and pesto *appetizers*
Guinea fowl with apples
Figs with cheese

Autumn Menu 10
Roast pepper salad
Moroccan chicken and olives with preserved lemon
Cracked wheat pilaff
Mango sorbet

Autumn Menu 11
Cannellini beans with tuna
Pasta with olives
Coffee and cheese pudding

Autumn Menu 12
Fried goat's cheese
Stuffed sweet peppers
Orange salad

Autumn Menu 1

*Mushrooms stuffed with snails
or mussels
Rabbit with prunes
Potatoes with celeriac
Black grapes white cheese*

Two of the dishes for this autumn menu were given to me by friends. The stuffed mushrooms come from Monique Fabre who lives in France. She had been out to lunch and when she next saw me she enthused over the starter. It was a simple dish of field mushrooms, stuffed with snails, topped with garlic butter. I couldn't wait to try it out. It was as delicious as she promised and I discovered that when I couldn't get hold of snails, it worked just as well using canned mussels. It can be put together at any convenient moment during the day and is baked just before the meal. (The butter is most easily softened in a microwave for 30 seconds, or in a bowl standing in hot water.) Don't forget to hand round French or Italian bread to mop up the buttery juices.

Rabbit with prunes is a famous combination but this quick and easy way of preparing it was given to me by another friend, Ingrid Danckwerts, expressly for this book. She in turn gives the credit to a French friend, who is a poet and a count (though in which order I do not know). Wine, prunes, rabbit and bacon combine to give the dish a rich sweetness which goes beautifully with a green salad and mashed potatoes with celeriac; or you could serve steamed or boiled potatoes dusted with chopped parsley or sweet basil. The dish needs 1½ hours to cook, so you may prefer to make it the day before and reheat it half an hour or so before the meal. If buying a whole rabbit get the butcher to cut it into pieces for you, and if its liver is available, add it 5 minutes before the end of cooking time. The prunes can be pitted or not, it's up to you. Mash the potatoes and celeriac together just before you sit down to the starter and keep them warm in the oven.

The meal ends with a black and white platter of grapes and

cheese which you can arrange an hour or so before the guests arrive. Make sure to include some creamy fromage frais or Italian mascarpone for the grapes to be dipped into. Serve with Bath Olivers or oatmeal biscuits and perhaps some unsalted butter.

Mushrooms Stuffed with Snails or Mussels

450–750 g (1–1½ lb) flat mushrooms

225 g (8 oz) can snails or mussels in brine, drained

100–150 g (4–5 oz) butter, softened

4 cloves garlic, chopped

squeeze of lemon juice

pinch of grated nutmeg

handful parsley, chopped

1 teaspoon dried thyme or 2 of fresh

salt

freshly milled black or mixed pepper

2–3 tablespoons breadcrumbs (see p. 183)

Can be prepared several hours ahead: Butter a shallow oven-proof dish and lay the mushrooms in it, stalk-side up. Arrange a few snails or mussels around each stalk. Mash the butter with the garlic, lemon juice, nutmeg, parsley, thyme, salt and pepper. Spread a dollop over each mushroom and sprinkle with the breadcrumbs.

To cook: Heat the oven to Gas 7/425°F/220°C and bake for 15–20 minutes.

Rabbit with Prunes

2 tablespoons flour

1 rabbit, cut in 8 pieces, or 900 g (2 lb) rabbit portions

4 tablespoons olive oil

150 g (6 oz) streaky bacon, chopped

150 g (6 oz) large prunes

300 ml (½ pint) dry white wine or dry cider

salt

freshly milled black pepper

Can be prepared a day ahead: Put the flour into a plastic or paper bag, add the rabbit pieces and shake well to coat them. Heat the oil in a flame-proof casserole and brown the meat all over, in 2 or

3 batches as necessary. Remove to a plate. Fry the bacon pieces until just beginning to turn golden. Return half the rabbit to the casserole, add the prunes, and top with remaining rabbit. Add wine or cider and season with salt and pepper. Bring to the boil, cover and simmer for 1 hour; remove lid and simmer for a further 30 minutes.

Potatoes with Celeriac

750 g (1½ lb) potatoes   salt
750 g (1½ lb) celeriac   freshly milled black pepper
50 g (2 oz) butter   chopped parsley
2 or 3 tablespoons milk

To cook: Peel potatoes and celeriac and cut them into uniform pieces. Put them in a pan of salted water, bring to the boil and simmer until soft, 20–25 minutes. Drain well. Mash them with half the butter and the milk and season with salt and pepper. Put them in a dish, fork the surface, dot with the remaining butter and put them in the oven at Gas 4/350°F/180°C until ready to eat.
To serve: Dust with chopped parsley.

Black Grapes White Cheese

450 g (1 lb) black grapes   white Stilton, etc, and
selection of white cheeses,   including fromage frais or
   such as goat's, Brie,   mascarpone
   Camembert, Coutances,

Can be prepared 1–2 hours ahead: Arrange grapes and cheese on a large platter.

Autumn Menu 2

Artichoke hearts with tomatoes
Tunisian lamb with dried fruit
Black and white rice
Honey-glazed pears

The meal begins with a light and delicious salad made with the last of the season's tomatoes and artichoke hearts preserved in oil, which are sold in Italian delicatessens and some supermarkets. If you can only find the canned variety, drain and rinse them well before adding the dressing, allowing an hour or so for them to absorb the flavours before adding the tomatoes and serving.

The main course is a simple peasant dish based on a Tunisian recipe, *sikbadj*. It can be eaten the day it is made, but like most stews, it adapts well to being made a day or so ahead and reheated. Make it with pitted dates and naturally dried apricots, sold in health-food or Asian shops, which will probably be from Afghanistan. They may not be as pretty as the bright orange ones, which are treated with sulphur to preserve their colour, but have a more pronounced and sweeter flavour. Some are dried unpitted, but if your guests are forewarned nobody seems to mind, though you can stone them if you prefer. The stew with its aubergines and chickpeas is a complete meal, and needs only to be served with rice: either plain, or a mixture of white and so-called wild rice with its long black grains. Wild rice is really a grass reed grown in Asia and North America, where the Red Indians were given the exclusive right to market it. It is expensive, but a small amount is visually appealing when added to white rice. You can buy white and black rice ready mixed – follow cooking instructions on the packet. If you want to serve a salad, you could offer sliced fennel dressed with lemon juice, walnut oil, salt and pepper.

Honey-glazed pears fill the kitchen with a mouthwatering smell, and they come out of the oven glazed in a syrupy sauce combining honey, butter and cream with a dash of spirits which could be calvados or brandy, or better still the famous pear liqueur, Poire William. Prepare them an hour or two before the supper.

Artichoke Hearts with Tomatoes

1 jar or can artichoke hearts
oil from the jar or olive or
  walnut oil
juice of 1 lemon
1 clove garlic, chopped
1 teaspoon capers

freshly milled black pepper
450 g (1 lb) ripe tomatoes,
  chopped
salt
handful chopped parsley or
  sweet basil

Can be prepared an hour or two ahead: Quarter the artichoke hearts and put them into a bowl with the oil from the jar, or sprinkle with olive or walnut oil. Add lemon juice, garlic, capers and black pepper.
To serve: Add the chopped tomatoes and mix carefully. Season with salt and garnish with the chopped parsley or sweet basil.

Tunisian Lamb with Dried Fruit

2 tablespoons oil
2 onions, chopped
750 g (1½ lb) braising or
  stewing lamb, cut in cubes
2 tablespoons tomato purée
1 cinnamon stick or 1
  teaspoon powdered
1 teaspoon allspice
salt
freshly milled black pepper

150 ml (¼ pint) water
225 g (8 oz) dates or dried
  apricots, or a mixture of
  the two
750 g (1½ lb) aubergines,
  cubed
1 can chickpeas, drained
handful chopped fresh
  coriander leaves or parsley

Can be prepared a day or several hours ahead: Heat the oil in a flameproof casserole and cook the onions until soft. Add the meat and brown all over. Stir in the tomato purée and season with the cinnamon, allspice, salt and pepper, add the water, bring to the boil and simmer until the meat is tender, 1½–2 hours.

Meanwhile, put the apricots, if you are using them, in a bowl and cover with boiling water. Put the cubed aubergines into a colander and sprinkle with salt. When the lamb is tender, rinse the aubergines under the cold tap and stone the apricots if necessary. Stir the aubergines, dates and or apricots, tomato purée and chickpeas into the pot. At this point continue the cooking or set aside until nearer the meal.

To continue cooking: Bring to the boil and simmer for a further 35–40 minutes. Taste and adjust seasoning. Garnish with the chopped coriander or parsley.

Black and White Rice

1 tablespoon oil	50 g (2 oz) wild rice
1 onion, chopped	salt
250 g (8 oz) long-grain white rice	1 whole clove garlic
	600 ml (1¼ pint) water

To cook: Heat the oil in a saucepan and fry the onion for a few minutes. Stir in both kinds of rice and cook for a moment or two. Add salt, the whole garlic clove and the water. Bring to the boil, cover and simmer for 25 minutes. Turn off the heat and leave to infuse for at least 10 minutes.

Honey-glazed Pears

4–6 pears, peeled and halved	2 tablespoons calvados, brandy or pear liqueur
juice of ½ lemon	
2–3 tablespoons honey	150 ml (¼ pint) crème fraîche
50 g (2 oz) butter	(see p. 187)
1 teaspoon cinnamon	

Can be prepared an hour or two ahead: Butter an oven-proof dish and lay the pears in it, cut-side down, in a single layer. Sprinkle with the lemon juice and spread each half with honey. Dot with the butter and sprinkle over the cinnamon. Set aside until ready to cook.

To cook: Heat the oven to Gas 4/350°F/180°C and bake for 20 minutes. Remove from the oven, sprinkle with the spirit and stir the crème fraîche into the hot juices. Return to the oven for another 20 minutes.

Autumn Menu 3

Baby corn with garlic butter
Steak tartare
Potato galette
Pumpkin pie

Cobs of baby corn are quick to cook and can be speared with cocktail sticks from a bowl set in the middle of the table. They should be soft but chewy, and served with French or Italian bread to mop up the juices. If you can't find baby corn, buy the fully-grown variety and serve with the same garlicky sauce. They take longer to cook – first strip them of their outer leaves and silky fibres, then boil for 15–20 minutes. Whichever kind you use, don't add salt to the cooking water, as it hardens them.

We used to eat steak tartare in a bar in Lausanne, where it was followed by a large platter of crisp French fries. It turned what might have been a bizarre dish (after all it is raw meat) into something quite simple and homely. If you are expert at making chips, you might like to copy this example, cutting the potatoes rather thinner than usual. Otherwise offer a potato galette, which needs less attention. Serve also a crisp green salad flavoured with a mustardy dressing. Steak tartare takes only minutes to prepare, and most of the work is done at table, as everyone mixes in their egg yolk and oil and adds vinegar, mustard, salt and pepper to taste. The dish is rich so calls for only a small amount of meat, which must be lean and very fresh because it is eaten raw. Try to avoid flavouring the dish with strongly pungent onions: use instead the milder shallots or red-skinned onions, neither of which will leave a lingering taste in the mouth.

Pumpkins appear around Hallowe'en and then disappear from all but ethnic shops. They keep for ages, especially if you buy them slightly green, when they will ripen over a period of weeks to bright orange. Their drawback is that in almost all recipes they need to be peeled, deseeded and cooked before they can be used. This problem can be partially solved by cooking more than you need and freezing the pulp for another time. Or you can use canned pumpkin pulp, which has suddenly appeared in our supermarkets. This pie can be prepared several hours ahead and put into the oven 35–40 minutes before it is to be eaten. It could be made without pastry in a buttered shallow dish – when it would need another name, pumpkin flan perhaps.

Baby Corn with Garlic Butter

450 g (1 lb) baby corn
150 g (6 oz) butter
1–2 cloves garlic, chopped
½ teaspoon soy sauce

freshly milled black pepper
French or Italian bread
cocktail sticks

To cook: Steam the baby corn for 10 minutes or boil for 5. Melt the butter with the garlic, soy sauce and pepper in a saucepan. Tip in the drained, cooked corn and toss for a few minutes over a medium heat.
To serve: Turn into a warm bowl and serve with the bread and the cocktail sticks to hand.

Steak Tartare

450 g (1 lb) fillet, sirloin or
   topside beef, minced
4 egg yolks
handful chopped parsley
4 shallots, or 1 mild onion,
   chopped
1 jar miniature gherkins,
   chopped

2 tablespoons capers, rinsed
   and chopped
olive oil
wine vinegar
Dijon mustard
salt
freshly milled black pepper

To prepare: Divide the meat between 4 dinner plates. Shape into rounds and flatten them. Make a hollow in the centre of each.

Separate the eggs – save the whites for something else – and put an egg yolk into each hollow. Sprinkle with chopped parsley and garnish with small mounds of chopped shallots, gherkins and capers.

To serve: Let everyone mix meat, egg and garnish and add oil, vinegar, mustard, salt and pepper to taste.

Potato Galette

25 g (1 oz) butter
450 g (1 lb) potatoes, peeled and cut in matchstick strips
salt

freshly milled black pepper
1–2 cloves garlic, chopped or crushed
handful parsley, chopped

To cook: Heat the oven to Gas 6/400°F/200°C. Melt the butter in a small frying pan with a heatproof handle, or a sandwich tin, turning it about to coat the sides. Add the potatoes, pressing them down. Add salt, pepper, garlic and parsley. Cover with foil and a lid. Cook on the stove over medium heat until the cake is golden underneath, 10–15 minutes. Test by lifting the edge with a spatula, and take care it does not burn. Transfer to the oven for 30 minutes. It will keep warm in the turned-off oven.

To serve: Invert a plate over the pan and turn it over so that the cake falls on to the plate. Take care not to burn yourself.

Pumpkin Pie

900 g (2 lb) pumpkin, weighed before peeling, or 450 g (1 lb) can pumpkin purée
salt
225 g (8 oz) block puff pastry, defrosted
2 eggs
150 ml (5 fl oz) single cream

100 g (4 oz) vanilla sugar (see p. 186) or caster sugar and a few drops vanilla essence
$\frac{1}{2}$ teaspoon cinnamon
grated nutmeg
juice of $\frac{1}{2}$ lemon
single cream or yogurt

Prepare several hours ahead: If using fresh pumpkin, peel, deseed and roughly chop. Place in a pan with a pinch of salt, cover with water and simmer for 10–15 minutes until soft. Drain in a colander and leave to cool. Either mash it or blend in a food processor until smooth. Roll out the pastry and use to line a greased 20 cm (8 in) flan tin.

To assemble and cook pie: Heat the oven to Gas 6/400°F/200°C. Blend or beat all other ingredients one at a time into the pumpkin purée. Pour into the pastry shell and bake for 35–40 minutes until the centre is cooked: test by inserting a skewer. The pie will keep warm quite happily in the turned-off oven.

To serve: Serve the cream or yogurt separately.

Autumn Menu 4

Sardines with Italian toast
Pheasant with mushrooms
Garlic fanned potatoes
Upside-down apple tart

Ordinary canned sardines are comforting served on buttered toast, and the boneless ones packed in olive oil are even better. Whichever you choose, they become something of a feast eaten with bread toasted the Italian way, *bruschetta*. Use Italian bread if you can find it, otherwise French bread or a loaf of any good quality country-style bread. The toast is browned in the oven and served with cut cloves of garlic and olive oil. Everyone sits down at the table and deals with their own, rubbing the toast with garlic, sprinkling it with oil and finally topping it with a sardine or two.

Game birds and mushrooms are two of the hunter's prizes and there are many country recipes in which they combine. In this one, a pheasant is cut into portions so there is no carving to be done at the table. The same recipe can be used for pigeons, but cut them in half and double the cooking time. Serve the pheasant with either watercress or sliced chicory topped with sliced oranges, (see pp. 106 and 109). The fanned potatoes can be peeled or not, it's up to you, and how much time you have.

The meal ends with a quick and foolproof way of making a famous apple tart, *tarte des demoiselles Tatin*. Instead of caramelizing the top at the end as most recipes suggest, it is done first and the whole thing can be assembled at any time during the day so that all you have to do at the supper is to bake it and turn it out. The fruit will be a deep amber with a spicy flavour. The recipe also works using pears or peaches. The pears can be flavoured with a little crumbled blue cheese and the peaches with flaked almonds. I suggest that you use a square of ready-rolled puff pastry in which case you'll need a 20 cm (8 in) sponge tin, but of course you can always roll out your own pastry and use whatever size tin you already own.

Sardines with Italian Toast

2 cans sardines in oil, drained
bunch of watercress
fresh sprigs of dill or fennel
lemon quarters
8–12 slices of Italian or
    French bread

6 garlic cloves, cut in half
olive oil
salt
freshly milled black pepper

Can be prepared ahead: Arrange the sardines on a small platter and garnish with the watercress, dill or fennel and lemon quarters. Put the garlic cloves in a small bowl.
To cook: Heat the oven to Gas 7/425°F/220°C. Put the slices of bread on a baking sheet and bake until golden.
To serve: Let everyone rub the toasted bread with garlic, sprinkle it with oil and add sardines, salt, pepper and lemon juice.

Pheasant with Mushrooms

50 g (2 oz) butter
1 pheasant, divided into 4
   portions
2 onions, chopped
350 g (12 oz) flat mushrooms,
   sliced
1 tablespoon tomato purée

salt
freshly milled black pepper
2 or 3 sprigs of fresh
   rosemary or 1 teaspoon
   dried thyme
150 ml (¼ pint) red or dry
   white wine

To cook: Melt the butter in a flameproof casserole and brown the pheasant portions all over, in 2 batches if necessary, then put them on a plate. Add the onions and mushrooms and let them soften for about 5 minutes, turning them from time to time. Stir in the tomato purée. Return the pheasant pieces, season with salt and pepper, add the rosemary or thyme and pour in the wine. Let it bubble, then cover and simmer for 45 minutes. Remove the lid and simmer for 15 minutes more to reduce the sauce.

Garlic Fanned Potatoes

8 baking potatoes, weighing
   approx. 100 g (4 oz) each
olive oil

salt
freshly milled black pepper
2 cloves garlic, chopped

To cook: Heat the oven to Gas 7/425°F/220°C. Oil a baking sheet. Lay the potatoes on the sheet and slice them almost to the base at 5 mm (¼ in) intervals, leaving a sufficient margin for the potato to hold together. Sprinkle with olive oil, salt and pepper. Bake for 1 hour. Ten minutes before they are ready, sprinkle them with more oil and the garlic.

Upside-down Apple Tart

100 g (4 oz) granulated sugar
50 g (2 oz) butter
1 tablespoon water
450 g (1 lb) Cox's or other
   eating apples, peeled and
   sliced
1 teaspoon cinnamon

grated nutmeg
1 sheet ready-rolled frozen
   puff pastry, defrosted
fromage frais, single cream,
   yogurt or crème fraîche
   (see p. 187)

Can be prepared several hours ahead: Put the sugar, half the butter and the water into a flan tin and heat gently on the stove until the sugar dissolves. Raise heat and cook until the mixture turns a deep gold. Remove from heat. Lay the apple slices on top, sprinkle with cinnamon and nutmeg and dot with remaining butter. Lay the pastry on top and tuck in the sides. Refrigerate until ready to cook.

To cook: Heat the oven to Gas 7/425°F/220°C. Bake for 30–35 minutes until the pastry is golden. The tart can be kept warm in the switched-off oven with the door ajar.

To serve: Carefully invert on to a serving plate, watching that the juice does not overflow. Serve the fromage frais, single cream, yogurt or crème fraîche separately.

Autumn Menu 5

*Prawns with mushrooms
and anchovies
Moroccan baked grey mullet
Fruit pancakes*

The quick to assemble starter must be prepared at least 1–2 hours ahead so that the anchovies can give pungency to the cultivated mushrooms and prawns. If these last are frozen, don't forget to give them several hours to defrost: trying to do this in the microwave doesn't give them a chance and ruins what flavour they have.

Grey mullet is both cheap and delicious, yet it is an under-valued fish. Make absolutely certain the fishmonger cleans it properly, emphasizing he should remove the long gut and gills and scale it properly, otherwise you will be landed with this messy chore. Ask him also to score the fish 2–3 times on either side. The fish will absorb the spicy flavours if you prepare it at least one or several hours ahead. Serve it with naan bread, wrapped in foil and warmed for 5–10 minutes in the oven, and a fresh salad.

Every child learns how to make pancakes, but they take up precious time. Solve the problem by using the excellent, ready-cooked crêpes or pancakes which are sold in packets by super-markets and delicatessens. The apples or pears must first be stewed in lemon juice, butter, sugar and cinnamon. This takes about 20 minutes but it can be done well ahead of time and the pancakes filled and set aside until you are ready to heat them.

Prawns with Mushrooms and Anchovies

225 g (8 oz) field mushrooms,
   sliced thinly
juice of 1 lemon
6–8 tablespoons olive oil
1 clove garlic, chopped
freshly milled mixed
   peppercorns or black
   pepper

225 g (8 oz) shelled prawns
50 g (2 oz) can anchovy
   fillets, drained and chopped
handful parsley, chopped

Prepare at least one to two hours ahead: Put sliced mushrooms into a serving bowl and sprinkle them with the lemon juice and 6 tablespoons olive oil. Add chopped garlic and season gener-ously with the pepper.

To serve: Mix in the prawns and chopped anchovies and if necessary add remaining olive oil. Garnish with the parsley.

Moroccan Baked Grey Mullet

1 kg (2¼ lb) grey mullet	salt
1 teaspoon cumin powder	juice of 2 lemons
1 teaspoon chilli powder	2 tablespoons olive oil
2 teaspoons paprika	1 can Italian chopped
2 cloves garlic, crushed	tomatoes
2 tablespoons fresh chopped	handful black olives
coriander or parsley	

Prepare one and up to several hours ahead: Lay the fish in a shallow china or glass dish. Mix the cumin and chilli powders with the paprika, garlic and chopped coriander or parsley. Rub this mixture well into the fish. Season with salt, add the juice of 1 lemon and the olive oil. Leave to marinate for at least 1 hour. **To cook:** Heat the oven to Gas 6/400°F/200°C. Pour the tomatoes over the fish, add juice from second lemon and the black olives. Cover with foil or buttered paper. Bake for 25–35 minutes. Test by inserting a skewer into the thickest part: the flesh should lift easily from the bone. If not, give it an extra few minutes.

Fruit Pancakes

450 g (1 lb) ripe eating apples or pears, peeled, cored and sliced	½ teaspoon cinnamon
	2 tablespoons chopped walnuts
1 tablespoon lemon juice	1 packet of 6 pancakes
50 g (2 oz) butter	1 tablespoon calvados, pear
75 g (3 oz) soft brown sugar	liqueur or brandy

Can be prepared several hours ahead: Put the sliced fruit into a frying pan. Add the lemon juice, half the butter, and the sugar and cinnamon. Cook gently until the slices are soft, turning them from time to time – about 20 minutes. Stir in the chopped walnuts. Open each pancake into a semi-circle (pancakes in packets are folded into 4) and place some of the filling on each. Roll them up and put them into a buttered oven dish. Pour over the buttery juices from the pan and dot with the remaining butter.

To cook: Heat the oven to Gas 4/350°F/180°C. Bake for 10–15 minutes. They can be kept warm in the turned-off oven with the door ajar.

To serve: Sprinkle with the spirit.

Autumn Menu 6

Pear and walnut salad
Toulouse sausages with garlic
Italian coffee cheese

Pears flavoured with walnuts make a light starter to a hearty meal of sausages. A good choice for the bonfire season perhaps. Prepare the salad up to an hour ahead. To ring the changes, use olive oil and olives instead of the walnut oil and walnuts.

Toulouse sausages, spicy and full of flavour, are sold in delicatessens and specialist shops. If you can't get them, choose the best quality herb or spicy sausages you can find: this French recipe transforms even the humblest kind into a far from humble dish. While they are cooking with onions and tomatoes, a dozen whole garlic cloves are simmered until soft and then added to the pan. This way of cooking garlic renders it sweet and soft and it is easily dealt with at table as everyone squashes their own with a fork until the soft purée oozes on to the plate. The dish won't spoil if the timetable goes askew and the cooking period has to be extended. Serve the sausages with either mashed or baked jacket potatoes; the latter will take about an hour at Gas 6/400°F/200°C, but if they have to be kept warm, prevent the skins from toughening by putting them in a dish and cover it with foil. If you're expecting hearty appetites, open 1–2 cans of flageolet or haricots beans and heat them through with a sprig of sage.

The meal ends with an Italian do-it-yourself dessert. The uninitiated may need a bit of coaxing because everyone helps themselves to what they want of the sugar and finely ground coffee, stirring them into the cheese before adding a dash of rum or amaretto.

Pear and Walnut Salad

4 ripe eating pears, peeled
   and sliced
juice of 1 lemon
freshly milled black pepper

4 or 5 tablespoons walnut oil
handful chopped walnuts
sprigs of watercress

Can be prepared an hour or so ahead: Arrange pear slices on
4 plates. Sprinkle with lemon juice and pepper. Moisten with
walnut oil, and garnish with chopped walnuts and watercress.

Toulouse Sausages with Garlic

12 cloves garlic
1 tablespoon olive oil
450–750 g (1–1½ lb)
   Toulouse, herb or spicy
   sausages
3 onions, sliced

1 can chopped tomatoes
½ teaspoon dried thyme
½ teaspoon dried oregano
freshly milled black pepper
salt

To cook: Put whole unpeeled garlic cloves into a saucepan, cover
with water and boil for 20 minutes. Heat the oil in a heavy-based
frying pan and brown the sausages all over, then remove and
brown the onions. Return sausages to the pan, pour in the canned
tomatoes and add thyme, oregano, pepper and a little salt to taste.
Simmer, uncovered, for 20 minutes, stirring occasionally. Add
the drained, whole garlic cloves and simmer for 10 minutes more.

Italian Coffee Cheese

450 g (1 lb) mascarpone or
   soft ricotta cheese
bowl of finely ground
   expresso or continental
   coffee

bowl of caster sugar
rum or amaretto

Can be done ahead: Spoon cheese into individual bowls.
To serve: Let everyone help themselves, mixing coffee, sugar and
rum or amaretto to taste into their cheese.

Autumn Menu 7

Mussels in cider
Mushrooms with bacon and pasta
Watercress and orange salad
Blackberry autumn pudding

This is a supper for those who enjoy talking while they are cooking, as much of it is prepared in front of the guests. Give everyone a glass of wine while the mussels are steaming and you are preparing the pasta sauce. The pasta goes into the pot a couple of minutes before you sit down to eat.

Mussels in cider is the Breton version of *moules marinières*. It's important that you use a strong dry cider, as sweet would ruin the flavour. People often balk at buying mussels, fearing they are difficult to clean. The opposite is true, but it's a good idea to buy them the day before because they virtually clean themselves if left to soak for several hours with a tablespoon of flour or bran. As they open to feed, they discard any lurking particles of sand. All that is then needed is a scrub under a running tap and a quick wash in 2–3 changes of cold water. When buying mussels don't let the fishmonger palm you off with a lot that are opened, as they may well be dead and therefore uneatable.

The simple pasta dish which follows is especially good if you are lucky enough to have a source of freshly picked wild mushrooms. Otherwise use the best you can find, such as shiitake, oyster or chestnut varieties, or the large field mushrooms which are meatier and have more flavour than the button variety. The sauce can be served with all sorts of pasta but spiral-shaped fusilli holds it nicely. The watercress salad is quick to prepare and can be made an hour or so ahead.

Blackberry autumn pudding, which is a variation on the traditional summer pudding, ends the meal but should be the first job you tackle as it improves the longer it sits, which can be up to 3 days. The apples should be a Cox's or any other firm, sweet variety.

Mussels in Cider

1 kg (2¼ lb) fresh mussels
1 tablespoon sea salt
1–2 tablespoons flour or bran
2 or 3 shallots, chopped
freshly milled black pepper
150 ml (¼ pint) strong dry
   cider

handful parsley, chopped
50 g (2 oz) butter, cut in
   pieces
French or Italian bread

Prepare several hours ahead or night before: Put mussels in a bowl or bucket of cold water with the salt and flour or bran. Leave for several hours.

To clean: Scrub the mussels under running cold water, and pull off the beards. Wash in 2 or 3 changes of water. Tap sharply with a wooden spoon any that are open; if they do not close, discard them, along with any that have broken shells. Leave cleaned mussels in a bowl of water until ready to cook.

To cook: Put shallots, pepper and cider into a large flameproof casserole that can be brought to the table. Add the mussels, cover and bring to the boil. Boil until the mussels have opened and are piping hot, for about 5 minutes. Add parsley and butter.

To serve: Serve from the casserole into soup bowls and provide a bowl for the discarded shells. Serve the bread separately.

Mushrooms with Bacon and Pasta

5 tablespoons olive oil
100 g (4 oz) streaky bacon,
   chopped
2 shallots, chopped
750 g (1½ lb) mushrooms,
   sliced
½ teaspoon dried thyme
salt

freshly milled black pepper
225–350 g (8–12 oz) fusilli
   pasta
4 tablespoons crème fraîche
   (see p. 187)
1 tablespoon garlic, chopped
generous handful chopped
   parsley

To make the sauce: Heat 4 tablespoons oil in a large frying pan and fry the bacon until all the fat runs, add the shallots and cook

until they are soft but brown. Add the mushrooms, turning them over and over to mix thoroughly with the bacon and shallots. Sprinkle in the thyme, salt and pepper. Lower the heat and cover the pan with foil or a lid. Continue cooking for 10–15 minutes.
To cook the pasta: Bring a large pan of water to the boil, add salt and 1 tablespoon oil. Stir in the fusilli in one go and boil hard for 2 minutes. Cover, turn off the heat and leave for 10 minutes.
To serve: Uncover the mushrooms, raise the heat and stir in the crème fraîche; sprinkle on the garlic and parsley. Drain pasta and put it into a warm bowl. Pile the sauce on top.

Watercress and Orange Salad

bunch of watercress
2 oranges

juice of ½ lemon
olive oil

Can be prepared an hour or so ahead: Wash and dry watercress and put into a bowl. Skin oranges over a plate, removing all traces of pith. Slice and put on top of the watercress, pouring over the juice. Add the lemon juice and sprinkle lightly with olive oil.

Blackberry Autumn Pudding

450 g (1 lb) blackberries, washed
225 g (8 oz) eating apples, peeled, cored and sliced
150 g (6 oz) caster or vanilla sugar (see p. 186)

2 tablespoons water
5 mm (¼ in) slices one-day-old white bread, crusts removed
pouring cream or fromage frais

Prepare one to three days ahead: Put the blackberries and sliced apples into a saucepan with the sugar and water. Bring slowly to the boil and when the sugar has dissolved, boil fiercely for 5 minutes. Line the base and sides of a 600 ml (1 pint) pudding basin or soufflé dish with the bread, plugging any gaps with small pieces. Pour the fruit and juice into the middle. Cover with a layer of bread, cut to fit. Put a saucer on top and weight it down with

something heavy, such as a flat-iron or a couple of tins. Refrigerate for at least 1 day.

To serve: Run a knife round the edge and carefully turn the
pudding out on to a serving dish with a lip, taking care not to spill
any juice. Serve the cream or fromage frais separately.

Autumn Menu 8

Chestnut soup
Venison with olives
Chicory and orange salad
Apricot fool

Fresh chestnuts appearing in the shops conjure up visions of log
fires and the company of friends. It's a pity that they are so
tedious to peel because apart from being roasted, they make
wonderful soups. Canned unsweetened chestnut purée is the
perfect answer, turning this into a soup that can be prepared in an
odd moment up to a day ahead.

Like all large game, venison benefits from being marinated, in
this case 1–3 days, but it could be as much as a week. The long,
slow cooking of this recipe (which can also be used for hare
portions) for 4–5 hours ensures it is beautifully moist and tender.
If you prefer, cook it a day ahead and reheat at Gas 4/350°F/
180°C for half an hour. Offer a bowl of rowan or redcurrant jelly
or cranberry sauce and serve it simply with steamed or boiled
potatoes, sprinkled with parsley and a chicory and orange salad
which takes little time to put together. Make sure the chicory is
white and golden, as it turns green once exposed to light and
becomes very bitter.

The apricots for the fool need stewing and cooling, so it's a
good idea to make it the day before. Use any good quality dried
apricots, but for a really special flavour try and get the small dark
ones, sold in Asian or health-food shops, which are so sweet they
need no extra sugar. They come from Afghanistan and are
sometimes known as Hunza apricots. Don't be put off by their

withered appearance, which gives no hint of the spicy flavour laced with burnt sugar that is trapped inside them. The best ones still have their stones, which are easy to remove once the fruit is soaked. If there's no time to make a fool, serve the stewed apricots, flavoured with a dash of pear liqueur or brandy and a sprinkling of toasted flaked almonds. Hand a bowl of cream or fromage frais separately.

Chestnut Soup

2 tablespoons olive oil
4 rashers streaky bacon, chopped
2 onions, chopped
2 carrots, chopped
1 stick celery, chopped
450 g (1 lb) can unsweetened chestnut purée

bay leaf
1 litre (1¾ pints) water
salt
freshly milled black pepper
handful croûtons (see p. 183)

Can be prepared a day ahead: Heat the oil in a saucepan and add the bacon, onions, carrots and celery. Cover and allow to sweat for 10 minutes. Break up the chestnut purée with a fork and stir it into the pan, add the bay leaf and mix in the water. Bring to the boil and season to taste with salt and pepper. Simmer for 30–40 minutes and put through a blender or mouli-légumes.
To serve: Heat the soup and serve sprinkled with the croûtons.

Venison with Olives

750 g (1½ lb) venison, cut in bite-sized pieces
for the marinade:
  1 onion, chopped
  1 carrot, chopped
  2 whole cloves, garlic
  bay leaf

12 juniper berries, crushed
1 teaspoon peppercorns
2 sprigs of rosemary
3 tablespoons olive oil
2 tablespoons red wine vinegar
300 ml (½ pint) red wine

12 shallots, peeled
100 g (4 oz) pitted green
  olives

6 rashers streaky bacon
salt
freshly milled black pepper

Marinate one to three days ahead: Using an earthenware casserole with a lid, put in the meat, onion, carrot, garlic, bay leaf, juniper berries, peppercorns, rosemary, olive oil, vinegar and red wine. Leave to marinate for 1–3 days, turning the meat over twice each day.

To cook: Heat the oven to Gas 2/300°F/150°C. Stir the shallots and olives into the pot and lay the streaky bacon on top, season with salt and pepper, cover and cook for 4–5 hours.

Chicory and Orange Salad

3–4 heads chicory, wiped and
  sliced
2 oranges, peeled, pith
  removed and sliced
juice of 1 lemon

salt
freshly milled black pepper
walnut or hazelnut oil
handful parsley, chopped

To serve: Lay the sliced chicory in a dish, add the orange slices, discarding all pith and pips. Squeeze over the lemon juice, season with salt and pepper and sprinkle with sufficient oil to moisten the leaves. Garnish with the chopped parsley.

Apricot Fool

225 g (8 oz) dried apricots
juice of ½ lemon
6 tablespoons 8% fat fromage
  frais

6 tablespoons crème fraîche
  (see p. 187)
caster or vanilla sugar
  (see p. 186), to taste
almond fingers or amarettis

Prepare a day ahead: Cover apricots with boiling water and leave for 1 hour to swell and absorb some of the liquid. Remove stones if necessary. Put the fruit into a pan and add sufficient water just to cover. Bring to the boil and simmer for 5 minutes. Strain and boil the liquid hard until it reduces by half. Blend the fruit, reduced liquid and lemon juice. Blend in the fromage frais and crème fraîche. Taste and if necessary add sugar. Put into glasses or small bowls and refrigerate.

To serve: Serve with almond fingers or amarettis.

Autumn Menu 9

Olive and pesto *appetizers*
Guinea fowl with apples
Figs with cheese

Little moreish appetizers, made with bought Italian olive paste and *pesto*, can be prepared at any odd moment during the day and put into the oven just as the guests arrive. By the time coats are shed and everyone has sorted themselves out, the appetizers will be ready to be eaten either with pre-supper drinks, or with everyone sitting at the table with a glass of wine. If there's a hitch, they can be kept warm in the turned-off oven for a while.

Guinea fowl look quite small but they are very meaty and one will feed 4 people comfortably. In this Norman dish, *pintadeau aux pommes*, the bird is cooked in cider surrounded by apples flavoured with cinnamon. The cider should be strong and dry, as any other sort, even medium dry, is just too cloying. Serve the bird with watercress or perhaps a chicory and orange salad (see p. 109) and steamed potatoes sprinkled with plenty of chopped parsley (see p. 80). A pheasant or a chicken can be cooked in the same way.

Fresh figs are delicious served with a bowl of Italian mascarpone, ricotta or fromage frais. Make sure they are at room temperature and not eaten straight from the fridge. Either pile them on to a dish and let everyone help themselves, dipping the figs into the cheese, or if you have time try slicing them, sprinkling them with a little lemon juice and honey and leaving them to marinate for an hour or so. If fresh figs are not available, follow the recipe for dried figs at the end of this supper.

Olive and *Pesto* Appetizers

2 sheets ready-rolled frozen
    puff pastry, defrosted
2–3 teaspoons black olive
    paste
2–3 teaspoons *pesto*

2–3 teaspoons grated
    parmesan
sprinkling dried oregano and
    thyme
1 egg, beaten

Can be prepared several hours ahead: Mark each sheet of pastry
into 3 sections using the back of a knife. Spread the centre section
of one sheet with olive paste and a sprinkling of herbs. Fold over
one section and spread again with the paste and a further
sprinkling of herbs. Fold over the third section. Brush with beaten
egg and sprinkle with cheese. Cut into 4 squares and divide each
square into 4 triangles or, if you want bite-sized pieces, into 8.
Repeat with the second sheet of pastry, using *pesto* and omitting
the herbs. Lay the appetizers on a damp baking sheet, put into a
plastic bag and refrigerate until ready to cook.
To cook: Heat the oven to Gas 7/425°F/220°C. Bake until they are
puffed and golden, 10–15 minutes.

Guinea Fowl with Apples

25 g (1 oz) butter
1 tablespoon oil
450 g (1 lb) Cox's or sweet
    dessert apples, peeled,
    quartered and cored
½ teaspoon cinnamon

1 guinea fowl
salt
freshly milled black pepper
150 ml (¼ pint) dry cider
2 tablespoons crème fraîche
    (see p. 187)

Can be prepared ahead: Melt half the butter and oil in a heavy-
based casserole in which the bird will sit comfortably, and gently
fry the apple slices with the cinnamon for 5–10 minutes. Remove
to a bowl. Pour the cider into the pan and boil hard until reduced
to 2 or 3 tablespoons, pour over the apples. Wipe out the pan.
To complete cooking: Heat the remaining butter and oil. Brown
the guinea fowl all over. Return apples and cidery juices to the

pan and season with salt and pepper. Simmer covered for 50
minutes. Add the cream and cook 5 minutes more.
To serve: Serve the bird on a dish surrounded by the apples. Boil
the sauce hard for a few minutes to reduce then pour over the
bird.

Figs with Cheese

12–16 fresh or dried figs
juice of ½ lemon
3 tablespoons runny honey
2 or 3 sprigs thyme

150 ml (¼ pint) red wine
water to cover
500 g (1 lb) carton fromage
 frais

Prepare several hours ahead or day before: Put the figs, lemon
juice, honey, thyme, wine and enough water to cover into a
saucepan. Simmer until figs are soft; fresh will take about
10 minutes, dried up to 1 hour. Remove figs and place them
in a serving dish. Boil the sauce hard until it has reduced by half,
pour over the figs and leave to cool.
To serve: Serve the fromage frais separately.

Autumn Menu 10

*Roast pepper salad
Moroccan chicken and olives
with preserved lemon
Cracked wheat pilaff
Mango sorbet*

Jenny Fraser, a friend whose kitchen suppers are always a delight,
invented this roast pepper salad to please her children and
subsequently dozens of guests. Years ago they sat in her Swiss
uncle's farmhouse kitchen, politely eating things they didn't
really like, and all the time on the sideboard there gleamed a bowl
of brightly coloured roasted sweet peppers which they were
longing to try. Most pepper salads specify peeling the peppers,
which is a time-consuming business. Jenny does away with all

that and bakes the peppers with onions in a hot oven, basting them with a sauce made with olive oil, vinegar, sugar, garlic and tomato purée until the vegetables become slightly caramelized. It is a visually beautiful dish and absolutely delicious. Make it the day before or several hours ahead to allow time for it to cool. You can vary it as you will by garnishing it just before serving with black olives, a criss-cross of anchovies or perhaps some coarsely chopped tomatoes and a dusting of sweet basil, but try if you can to use all the different coloured peppers. If there's just no time to do anything, open a couple of jars of sliced peppers preserved in oil, *peperoni*, or use Spanish canned *pimientos*, slicing them finely and mixing with the dressing. Serve with plenty of crusty bread to mop up the juices.

The flavours of the Moroccan-inspired main course, *djej bil zeetoon*, are bitter-sweet and spicy, each one complementing without overpowering the others. Preserved lemons, which are much milder than fresh, can be bought in upmarket grocers, but it's easy to preserve your own (see p. 185) and they keep for ages. If you prefer, you can make the dish the day before and reheat it for half an hour at Gas 4/350°F/180°C. Moroccan chickens are tougher and scraggier than those we buy and so I have adapted the recipe with this in mind. I suggest a cracked wheat pilaff to accompany the dish, but it could just as well be plain boiled rice or warm naan bread.

The meal ends with a mango sorbet which could be one you buy, but it is very easy to make. Fresh mangoes are messy fruit to deal with, so this version uses the canned variety.

Roast Pepper Salad

150 ml (¼ pint) olive oil, plus 2–3 tablespoons
6–8 assorted coloured plump peppers, deseeded and sliced
2 onions, sliced
salt
freshly milled black pepper
1 tablespoon wine vinegar
1 tablespoon soft brown sugar
1 tablespoon tomato purée
2 cloves garlic, chopped

Can be prepared a day or two ahead: Heat the oven to Gas 7/ 425°F/220°C. Oil a shallow gratin dish and put in the sliced peppers and onions. Season with salt and pepper and sprinkle with 2 or 3 tablespoons oil. Roast for 20 minutes. Mix the 150 ml (¼ pint) oil, vinegar, sugar, tomato purée and garlic in a screw-top jar. Shake well and spoon over the peppers. Continue to roast for a further 30–50 minutes, stirring and basting every 10 minutes or so, until the onions and peppers just begin to caramelize. Set aside to cool. Cover and refrigerate.

To serve: Remove from fridge an hour or so before eating.

Moroccan Chicken and Olives with Preserved Lemon

100 g (4 oz) pitted green
  olives
3–4 tablespoons olive oil
4 chicken quarters, skinned
2 onions, chopped
1 teaspoon ground ginger
½ teaspoon turmeric
1 teaspoon cinnamon
3 cloves garlic, chopped or
  crushed

1 tablespoon tomato purée
150 ml (¼ pint) water
salt
freshly milled black pepper
handful fresh parsley,
  chopped
handful coriander, chopped
  or 1 teaspoon freeze-dried
peel of 1 preserved lemon,
  finely chopped (see p. 185)

Can be prepared a day ahead: Soak the olives in a bowl of water. Heat the oil in a heavy-based flameproof casserole and brown the chicken quarters, in 2 batches if necessary. Remove and keep warm. Add the onions and fry until golden. Stir in the ginger, turmeric, cinnamon and garlic. Cook a few minutes and mix in the tomato purée. Stir in the water and when the sauce bubbles, add salt, pepper, parsley and coriander. Return the chicken pieces and turn them over and over to coat them well. Cover, lower heat and simmer for 1 hour. Drain olives and add to the pan together with the finely chopped preserved lemon peel. Cook uncovered for a further 5 minutes and serve from the casserole.

Cracked Wheat Pilaff

2 tablespoons olive oil
1 clove garlic, chopped
25 g (1 oz) slivered almonds
225 g (8 oz) cracked or
  bulghur wheat

600 ml (1 pint) water
salt
freshly milled black pepper

To cook: Heat the oil in a saucepan and fry the garlic and almonds for 1 or 2 minutes, then stir in the cracked wheat and mix well. Pour in the water, bring to the boil and add salt and pepper. Cover and simmer for 15 minutes. Turn off the heat and leave for 5–10 minutes before serving.

Mango Sorbet

450 g (1 lb) can mangoes
2 tablespoons lime or lemon
  juice

2 tablespoons icing sugar
2 egg whites
almond biscuits or fan wafers

Prepare at least one day ahead: Purée the mangoes with their juice, the lime juice and icing sugar. Put into a shallow container and freeze until mixture begins to set. Beat the egg whites until stiff and fold into the mixture. Freeze again.

To serve: Scoop or spoon into bowls and serve the almond biscuits or wafers separately.

Autumn Menu 11

Cannellini beans with tuna
Pasta with olives
Coffee and cheese pudding

This supper begins with a fairly impromptu Italian starter, *fagioli con tonno*, which takes hardly any time to put together. The bland beans are sharpened with onion and lemon juice and topped with canned tuna. It can be made several hours ahead and refrigerated, but take it out an hour or so before you eat, as its much nicer if not icy cold. Serve it with Italian, French or pitta bread.

The Italian theme continues with a pasta dish which was given to me by my Sardinian friend Maria-Antonietta Pau. She makes it with gemelli, which is a pasta of short, double strands of spaghetti twisted together, designed to hold the sauce. I've made it with chiocciole, shaped like an open-work spiralling snail-shell. If you can't get hold of either, use another sort of spiral-shaped pasta such as fusilli or tortiglioni. There is no salt or pepper in the recipe because the bacon and olives are salty enough and in Sardinia they add pepper at the table. Either make the sauce just before the meal or make it ahead and reheat it while you cook the pasta. Follow the dish with a crisp green salad.

The dessert, *tiramisù*, is another of Maria-Antonietta's recipes which she sent to me in exchange for one for Christmas pudding. Hers is definitely much easier. It is made with sponge fingers, *mascarpone* or other cream cheese, separated eggs and strong coffee either in one large dish, or individual ones.

Cannellini Beans with Tuna

450 g (1 lb) can cannellini beans, drained
225 g (8 oz) can tuna in oil
1 clove garlic, chopped
juice of ½ lemon

1 red-skinned or other mild onion, thinly sliced
freshly milled black pepper
olive oil
handful chopped parsley

Can be prepared several hours ahead: Put the beans into a shallow serving bowl. Add the tuna with its oil, breaking it up with a fork, and mix well. Add garlic, lemon juice and the onion broken into rings. Season with black pepper and moisten with olive oil. Cover and refrigerate. Remove an hour ahead.
To serve: Sprinkle over the parsley.

Pasta with Olives

3 tablespoons olive oil
225 g (8 oz) streaky bacon,
   chopped
2 onions, chopped
2 cans Italian chopped
   tomatoes
2 tablespoons capers, rinsed
2 teaspoons sugar

handful fresh oregano or
   marjoram, chopped
350–450 g (12–16 oz) spiral-
   shaped pasta
400 g (14 oz) can pitted green
   olives, chopped coarsely
   (equivalent to 225 g (8 oz)
   when drained)

Sauce can be prepared several hours ahead: Heat 2 tablespoons
oil in a saucepan and fry the bacon and onions until just
beginning to brown. Add the tomatoes, capers, sugar, oregano or
marjoram. Simmer for 30 minutes, uncovered.

To cook pasta: Bring a large pan of salted water to the boil, add
the pasta and a tablespoon of oil, stir and boil fiercely for
2 minutes. Cover, turn off heat and leave for 10 minutes.

To serve: If made ahead, reheat the sauce. Add the olives and
leave them to heat through while you drain the pasta. Turn it into
a warm dish, add sauce and mix at the table.

Coffee and Cheese Pudding

150 ml (¼ pint) double
   strength coffee
2 eggs, separated
25 g (1 oz) sugar
2 tablespoons brandy or rum

250 g (10 oz) mascarpone or
   cream cheese
100 g (4 oz) sponge or
   boudoir biscuits
2–3 tablespoons cocoa

Prepare one day ahead: Make the coffee and set aside to cool.
Beat the egg yolks, sugar, brandy and cheese until creamy. Beat
the egg whites until they are firm and fold into the cheese mixture.
Dip the biscuits one by one into the coffee and use half to line a
deepish dish. Spread over half the cheese mixture. Make a second
layer with the remaining biscuits, dipping them into the coffee.
Pour over any remaining coffee and cover with the rest of the

cheese mixture. Sprinkle the cocoa all over the surface. Cover and chill till next day in the fridge.

Autumn Menu 12

Fried goat's cheese
Stuffed sweet peppers
Orange salad

Goat's cheeses coated in breadcrumbs are delicious fried. They can be prepared several hours ahead using home-made breadcrumbs, not the kind you buy in packets. If there's no time to prepare your own, you might find already breadcrumbed cheeses in some supermarkets, although of course they cost more. The rounds of cheese are fried in olive oil and garnished with black olives, but you can ring the changes by using walnut oil and chopped walnuts instead; or you could skip the garnish altogether and serve the fried cheeses with cranberry sauce or wild rowan jelly.

Sweet peppers, brought to Europe by the Spanish from South America, are now almost synonymous with Mediterranean and Middle Eastern cooking. Their shape makes them particularly suitable for stuffing and there are dozens of variations. Don't be put off by the long list of ingredients: this Persian version, *dolmeh felfel sabz*, is a complete meal in a pot. It can be put together hours ahead, but you must allow a good hour and a half for it to cook. In fact it reheats well, so you could make the whole thing the day before and reheat it either on top of the stove or in the oven for 30 minutes at Gas 4/350°F/180°C.

The dessert is easy to prepare and can be done well ahead. Peel the oranges in a spiral with a very sharp knife using a sawing action, cutting deep enough to remove the pith. If you've no time you could use 2 or 3 jars of whole mandarins. Don't slice them — simply empty into a serving bowl and flavour with the honey, lemon juice, cinnamon and orange-flower water. Sprinkle them at the last moment with almond flakes.

Fried Goat's Cheese

1 cylindrical or 2 round
   goat's cheeses 225 g (8 oz)
150 ml (¼ pint) milk
2–3 tablespoons dried breadcrumbs (see p. 183)
2 tablespoons olive oil

sprigs of watercress
2 tomatoes, sliced
handful black olives
freshly milled black pepper
1 tablespoon chopped fresh
   basil

Can be prepared several hours ahead: Cut the cylindrical goat's cheese into four rings or cut the round cheese in half round the middle. Dip the pieces in milk then into breadcrumbs, coating each side. Set aside.

To cook: Heat oil in a frying pan and fry the cheeses gently for 3–4 minutes on each side, until they are golden and the cheese is beginning to ooze.

To serve: Put on to 4 individual plates and garnish with watercress, tomatoes and olives. Season liberally with black pepper and sprinkle over any remaining oil and the chopped basil.

Stuffed Sweet Peppers

2 tablespoons olive oil
1 onion, chopped
225 g (8 oz) minced beef
2 tablespoons chopped fresh
   herbs such as coriander or
   oregano, or 2 teaspoons
   dried herbs
1 tablespoon chopped parsley
2 cloves garlic, chopped
1 teaspoon cinnamon
2 tablespoons tomato purée

4 tablespoons left-over
   cooked rice or fresh
   breadcrumbs
salt
freshly milled black pepper
4 bell-shaped sweet peppers
1 can chopped tomatoes
450–750 g (1–1½ lb) small
   new potatoes, scrubbed but
   not peeled
4 dessertspoons thick goat's
   or ewe's milk yogurt

Can be prepared several hours ahead: Use a heavy-based flame-proof casserole just big enough to hold the upright peppers comfortably. Heat the oil in it and fry the onion until soft and golden. And meat and let it brown and cook for 10–15 minutes, stirring occasionally. Stir in the herbs, parsley, garlic, cinnamon, tomato purée and rice or breadcrumbs. Season generously with salt and pepper. Cut tops off peppers, remove seeds and fill with the mixture. Empty the can of tomatoes into the casserole and stand the peppers on top. Put on their caps.

To cook: Bring to the boil, cover and lower heat. Cook for 30 minutes. Add the potatoes and continue cooking for a further 45–60 minutes, until peppers and potatoes are soft.

To serve: Remove caps and put a dollop of yogurt on each; return caps and serve.

Orange Salad

50 g (2 oz) flaked almonds
8 oranges, peeled and sliced
2 tablespoons orange-flower water

juice of $\frac{1}{2}$ lemon
2 or 3 tablespoons honey
2 teaspoons cinnamon

Can be prepared several hours ahead: Toast the almonds under the grill until golden brown. Put the sliced oranges into a bowl, discarding all pith and pips. Add orange-flower water, lemon juice and honey and sprinkle with the cinnamon.

To serve: Sprinkle with the toasted almonds.

Winter

Winter Menu 1
Courgette pots
Kidneys in wine
Braised chicory
Winter fruit salad

Winter Menu 2
Calabrese with black butter
Beef in red wine
Prune ice cream

Winter Menu 3
Garlic prawns
Quail with green olives
Flamed Alaska

Winter Menu 4
Goat's cheese on croûtons
Chicken with rosemary
Flageolets with crème fraîche
Dried fruit in red wine

Winter Menu 5
Avocado dip
Chilli beef and beans
Pineapple upside-down cake

Winter Menu 6
Artichokes with peas
Cottage pie
Braised cabbage with juniper
Cranberry winter pudding

Winter Menu 7
Pâté with onion jam
Trout parcels
Bread and butter pudding

Winter Menu 8
Potted prawns
Liver and onions
Marmalade apples

Winter Menu 9
Black olives, oranges and fennel
Chicken with honey
Creamy rice pudding

Winter Menu 10
Mushrooms in vine leaves
Pigeons with bitter orange
Chocolate chestnut cream

Winter Menu 11
Little mussel pots
Hare with juniper and prunes
Baked mushrooms
Caramel custard

Winter Menu 12
Chicory with croûtons
Breton fish casserole
The thirteen desserts

Winter Menu I

Courgette pots
Kidneys in wine
Braised chicory
Winter fruit salad

The idea for this first course was inspired by Viviane Slaski, a friend who is a naturally good cook. She makes everything seem easy, producing delightfully informal and unpretentious meals in her warm and friendly kitchen. These little courgette pots are like individual soufflés, with none of the terrors that word tends to arouse. On the contrary, they are extremely easy to make. You can do some of the work well ahead if you want, or put them together just before the meal. You could use prawns, canned mussels or asparagus spears instead of the courgettes, in which case there is no preliminary frying. If using parmesan, it's worth buying a small block, grating it and storing it in the freezer to be used as and when needed.

The kidneys in wine are quickly sautéed just before you sit down, and then left to simmer gently while the starter is eaten. They will be still slightly pink in the centre and very tender. Don't be tempted to lengthen the cooking time or you'll risk making them tough. Use lamb's kidneys, peeling away any of the thin outer membrane; split them in half and cut away the fatty core. Serve them with braised chicory and jacket potatoes.

The pretty fruit salad with which this supper ends was the inspiration of my husband's cousin, Valentine. It looked and tasted so delightfully refreshing, mixing tiny whole mandarins, white lychees and pale grapes with the startling green and black of kiwifruit, that I couldn't wait to make it myself. Prepare it at least an hour ahead, much longer if you wish, and refrigerate. Serve it with thick cream, fromage frais or Greek yogurt.

Courgette Pots

1 tablespoon butter
100 g (4 oz) courgettes, finely
  sliced
sprig of rosemary or
  ½ teaspoon dried thyme
2 eggs
4 tablespoons crème fraîche
  (see p. 187)

grated nutmeg
salt
freshly milled black pepper
4 teaspoons grated parmesan
  or mature cheddar

Can be prepared ahead: Melt the butter in a frying pan and fry the courgettes gently for 5 minutes with the rosemary or thyme. Remove and discard the rosemary. Butter 4 ramekin or cocotte pots and divide the courgettes and their buttery juices between them. Beat the eggs and add the crème fraîche; beat well and add grated nutmeg, salt and pepper.

To cook: Heat the oven to Gas 6/400°F/200°C. Beat the egg mixture again and pour it over the courgettes, leaving a margin of about 1 cm (½ in) below the top of each pot. Sprinkle over the cheese. Bake for 20–25 minutes until risen and golden.

Kidneys in Red Wine

50 g (2 oz) butter
1 tablespoon oil
2 onions, chopped
12 lamb's kidneys, halved and
  cored

salt
freshly milled black pepper
4 tablespoons red wine
handful chopped parsley
1 clove garlic, chopped

Cook just before the meal: Heat the butter and oil in a flameproof pan or dish that can be brought to the table. Fry the onion until soft, about 5 minutes. Add the kidneys and cook over a high flame, turning them over once or twice until the outsides are seared. Add salt, pepper and the red wine. Cover and lower the heat. Simmer very gently for 10–15 minutes.

To serve: Sprinkle with the parsley and garlic and bring to the table.

Braised Chicory

50 g (2 oz) butter
4 heads chicory
salt

juice of 1 lemon
handful chopped parsley

To cook: Melt the butter in a saucepan, add the chicory, salt and lemon juice. Cover and cook very gently until tender, shaking the pan from time to time, 8–10 minutes. Set aside to keep warm while you eat the starter. Serve dusted with chopped parsley.

Winter Fruit Salad

1 jar whole Spanish mandarin
  oranges
1 can lychees
225 g (8 oz) seedless green
  grapes

1–2 ripe kiwifruit, peeled and
  sliced
1–2 tablespoons orange-
  flower water

Prepare at least one or several hours ahead: Put the oranges and lychees with their syrup into a glass bowl. Mix in the grapes, arrange the sliced kiwis over the top and sprinkle with orange-flower water. Cover and refrigerate.

Winter Menu 2

Calabrese with black butter
Beef in red wine
Prune ice cream

Green or purple-headed calabrese, which is a variety of broccoli, is widely available and makes an inexpensive starter. It originated in Calabria in Sicily but is now extensively cultivated in other parts of Europe. It can be eaten like asparagus in the fingers and served as in this recipe with a black butter sauce, *beurre noire*, which in fact is not black at all but a walnut brown. Or if you prefer, it can be cooked ahead and eaten cold with either mayonnaise or a vinaigrette sauce, which is especially good if made with walnut, hazelnut or olive oil, flavoured with lemon juice, salt and pepper.

The beef dish comes from Greece where it is called *stifatho*. It is a glorious Mediterranean concoction which is slowly stewed until the meat and onions are meltingly tender. It needs no accompaniment other than mashed or baked jacket potatoes or perhaps plain boiled rice. It is child's play to prepare, as the meat is marinated overnight in the wide, earthenware pot in which it is to be cooked and served. The next day small, whole onions and tomatoes are added to the pot which then goes into a low oven for 4–5 hours. (The onions are easier to peel if you steep them for a few minutes in boiling water.) Use the same recipe for cubed pork, venison or even wild boar; or as a delicious and easy way to cook rabbit or hare portions.

Once tried, even the most anti-prune diehards become mad about this ice cream which comes from Agen in France. There, for centuries, they have been growing plums to make their famous prunes, dark and rich and full of sweet flavour. Fortunately, an enterprising Frenchman began growing the special trees in America, so the Californian prune which is so widely sold in this country is the same variety. To save having to stone them, buy large, pitted prunes and for a change try the same recipe with apricots. Make it a couple of days in advance, or much longer if you wish. But if you've allowed no time for that, blend the cooked prunes and their reduced liquid into a block or tub of softened vanilla ice cream (leave it out of the freezer for an hour or two) and return to the freezer to harden. Before serving the ice cream, take it out of the freezer half an hour before it is to be eaten and put it in the fridge. This process allows it to ripen and develop the flavour. Serve it with fan wafers and a sprinkling of spirits such as armagnac or brandy, or an orange-based liqueur or perhaps a spoonful or two of *Rumtopf* (see Alcoholic Fruits, p. 177).

Calabrese with Black Butter

750 g (1½ lb) calabrese or
   broccoli
salt
100 g (4 oz) butter
juice of ½ lemon

2 tablespoons capers,
   chopped
2 tablespoons chopped
   parsley
freshly milled black pepper

To cook: Trim the calabrese stalks into even-sized florets. Steam or boil them in a little water with salt until the stalks are tender, 15–20 minutes, then drain. Melt the butter in another pan and cook until it is nutbrown; remove from the heat, squeeze in the juice of the lemon, add the capers and parsley and season with pepper.

To serve: Arrange the calabrese on a platter with the buttery sauce in a bowl in the centre.

Beef in Red Wine

900 g (2 lb) chuck or braising
   steak, cut in 4 cm (1½ in)
   cubes
300 ml (½ pint) red wine
2 tablespoons red wine
   vinegar
2 tablespoons olive oil
1 teaspoon peppercorns
2 whole cloves

½ teaspoon allspice
24 pickling onions, peeled
1 can Italian chopped
   tomatoes, drained
1 tablespoon tomato purée
2 cloves garlic, chopped
bay leaf
salt

Prepare 24 hours ahead: Put the meat, red wine, vinegar, oil, peppercorns, cloves and allspice into an earthenware casserole with a well-fitting lid and leave overnight to marinate.

To cook: Heat the oven to Gas 3/325°F/160°C. Add onions, tomatoes, tomato purée, garlic, bay leaf and salt to the casserole, mix well, cover and bake for 3–4 hours.

Prune Ice Cream

225 g (8 oz) large pitted
  prunes
300 ml ($\frac{1}{2}$ pint) freshly made
  tea
100 g (4 oz) caster sugar

vanilla pod or cinnamon stick
thinly pared rind of $\frac{1}{2}$ lemon
300 ml ($\frac{1}{2}$ pint) fromage frais
300 ml ($\frac{1}{2}$ pint) double cream
wafers or chocolate whirls

Prepare at least 2 days ahead: Soak the prunes overnight in the tea
with the sugar, vanilla pod or cinnamon and lemon rind. Next
day transfer everything to a pan and simmer for 30 minutes.
Remove the prunes and blend them in a food processor. Boil the
liquid hard until only 3 tablespoons remain. Blend this with the
prunes. Add the fromage frais and blend again and finally blend
in the cream. Put into a shallow container and freeze for 2 hours.
Beat well and freeze for at least 24 hours. (Or if using an ice cream
maker, follow manufacturer's instructions.)
To serve: Remove from freezer and put into the fridge half an
hour before serving. Serve wafers or chocolate whirls separately.

Winter Menu 3

Garlic prawns
Quails with green olives
Flamed Alaska

The starter for this supper takes only minutes to prepare and is
perfect for the cook who likes to show off a little. The unshelled
prawns are tossed in butter and oil until hot through and then
flavoured with garlic, spices and parsley. If you buy them frozen,
let them defrost naturally, and don't be tempted to put them in
the microwave or in hot water, as it will ruin their flavour. At
table, everyone peels their own, so make sure you provide
fingerbowls and plenty of napkins. Offer a good supply of French
or Italian bread and put soy sauce and cayenne pepper on the
table.

The recipe for the quails comes from Languedoc and is

normally done with the very first of the olives, *olives cassées*, which are prepared and flavoured with fennel and orange at the beginning of winter when the crop is still green. It calls for peeled, deseeded and chopped tomatoes and the easiest and tastiest way of achieving this in winter is with the ever faithful canned Italian chopped tomatoes. The quails are first browned and then simmered with all the other ingredients for a short time. Serve them with plain boiled rice or a mixture of white and black (see p. 92). If the expected appetites are gargantuan, you had better offer 2 quails per head but more modest eaters will find one quite adequate.

The meal ends with a flourish, with the ice cream dessert brought flaming to the table. It is assembled hours or days ahead (the only strenuous bit is beating the egg whites) and is stored in the freezer before being put into a hot oven for a few minutes. You can use any sort of ice cream, from a simple vanilla to something more exciting like almond caramel, but whatever you choose, go for quality rather than cheapness. If there's just no time at all, simply pile ice cream on to a serving dish and flame it at the table either with brandy or, as they do in Brittany and Normandy, with a pear liqueur or calvados.

Garlic Prawns

25 g (1 oz) butter	juice of ½ lemon
4–5 tablespoons olive oil	½ teaspoon paprika
450 g (1 lb) prawns in their shells	1 teaspoon soy sauce
	cayenne pepper
4 cloves garlic, chopped or crushed	salt
	handful parsley, chopped

To cook: Heat the butter and oil in a frying pan and when it is sizzling, add the prawns and toss them over a high heat for 3 or 4 minutes. Add all the other ingredients and serve straight from the pan or pile on to a hot plate.
To serve: Have fingerbowls, plenty of napkins and a bowl in the centre for the shells. To eat the prawns, peel off legs and the shell

around the tail. Hold the prawn by the head and pull off the tail between your teeth, sucking out the juices. Discard the head. This may sound gruesome but it is exceedingly delicious!

Quails with Green Olives

100 g (4 oz) pitted green
  olives
50 g (2 oz) concentrated
  butter
4–8 quail
1 large onion, chopped
2 cloves garlic, chopped or
  crushed
several sprigs of parsley
1 teaspoon coriander seeds

bay leaf
piece of orange peel
sprig of dried fennel or
  1 teaspoon fennel seeds
1 can Italian chopped
  tomatoes
freshly milled mixed or black
  pepper
salt
bunch of watercress

To cook: Put the olives to soak in cold water. Melt the butter in a large flameproof casserole and brown the quail all over. Remove and add the onion and let it soften for a few minutes. Return the birds and add garlic, parsley, coriander seeds, bay leaf, orange peel, fennel and tomatoes. Season with pepper. Add the drained olives and simmer covered for 30 minutes. Taste and add salt if necessary.

To serve: Put quail on to a warm serving dish, surround with the sauce and garnish with watercress.

Flamed Alaska

450 g (1 lb) ice cream
1 small bought sponge flan
  case

3 tablespoons brandy
2 egg whites
50 g (2 oz) caster sugar

Prepare several hours or days ahead: Take the ice cream out of the freezer. Choose a shallow oven-proof dish that can go straight from the freezer into the oven. Lay the flan in it and sprinkle with 1 tablespoon of brandy. As soon as the ice cream is slightly soft, stir in a second tablespoon of brandy and spread the ice cream

over the flan, leaving a margin all round of about 1 cm (½ in).
Whip the egg whites until stiff, beat in the sugar a tablespoon at a
time, and pile over the ice cream, spreading right to the edges. Put
the alaska into the freezer until ready to cook. (The meringue
topping will remain slightly soft.)
To cook: Heat the oven to Gas 7/425°F/220°C. Put the alaska
straight from the freezer into the hot oven and cook for
3–5 minutes, until the top is golden brown. Put the third
tablespoon of brandy into a ladle or small saucepan, heat it and
pour it flaming over the meringue.

Winter Menu 4

Goat's cheese on croûtons
Chicken with rosemary
Flageolets with crème fraîche
Dried fruit in red wine

The idea for this warming starter, which can be prepared an hour
of so before the meal, comes from a French restaurant in the
Ardèche, l'Escarbille, where they call it simply *fromage chaud*.
They make it with their local goat's cheese and I follow suit by
using our Somerset or Welsh cheeses which in recent years have
come into the shops. Sometimes I use the plainest sort, at other
times I go for something fancier like ones rolled in citrus pepper
or herbs.

Rosemary is one of the few evergreen herbs, so it is particularly
useful in winter for dishes like this one from Italy, *pollo alla
rosmarino*. It can be made with chicken quarters, or with a whole
bird jointed with the aid of a sharp pair of kitchen shears.
Whichever you use, it's worth going for free-range or cornfed
chicken. The pieces are lightly browned in oil with the rosemary
before wine and whole cloves of garlic are added and it is left to
simmer for 45 minutes. At the end of this time, the garlic cloves
will be soft and swollen, the sweet purée ready to be squeezed out

on each plate with the back of a fork. Serve the dish with flageolet beans, plenty of crusty bread and a straightforward green salad.

The dried fruit in red wine, which is based on a Basque Christmas Eve recipe, *zurracapote*, is prepared at least one day ahead. It keeps for ages in a jar or in the fridge. The fruit is simmered for a short time in red wine, water, sugar and spices and then left to swell and absorb all the flavours. If you refrigerate it, remove it an hour or two ahead so that the fruits are not served at a freezing temperature. Variations on this salad are made elsewhere, including the Middle East, where they omit the wine and double the amount of water, flavouring the fruit salad at the last minute with a tablespoon or two of rose- or orange-flower water and a sprinkling of chopped pistachio nuts (not the salted kind) or almonds.

Goat's Cheese on Croûtons

olive oil
8 slices French bread
225 g (8 oz) cylindrical goat's
  cheese

bunch of watercress
freshly milled mixed or black
  pepper

Can be prepared an hour or so ahead: Oil a baking sheet and lay the bread slices on top. Cut the cheese into 8 rings and lay one on each slice of bread. Wash the watercress and use to line a serving platter or individual plates.
To cook: Heat the oven to Gas 7/425°F/220°C. Sprinkle the croûtons with olive oil. Bake 5–10 minutes until the bread is golden and the cheese bubbling. Arrange on the watercress and sprinkle with mixed or black pepper (omit if using citrus pepper cheese).

Chicken with Rosemary

2 tablespoons olive oil
2 or 3 sprigs rosemary
4 chicken quarters cut in half,

or 1 chicken divided into 8
  portions

150 ml (¼ pint) dry white
  wine
salt

freshly milled black pepper
8–12 unpeeled whole cloves
  garlic

To cook: Heat the oil in a heavy-based pan with the rosemary and fry the pieces of chicken until golden all over, in 2 batches if necessary. Remove the rosemary, return all the chicken pieces, pour in the wine, let it bubble and season with salt and pepper. Add the garlic, cover, lower the heat and cook gently for 45 minutes to 1 hour.

Flageolets with Crème Fraîche

1 can flageolets
25 g (1 oz) butter
2 tablespoons crème fraîche
  (see p. 187)

salt
freshly milled black pepper
handful chopped parsley

To cook: Empty the can of flageolets into a saucepan and heat gently. Drain, add butter, crème fraîche, salt and pepper and stir until hot through. Serve garnished with chopped parsley

Dried Fruit in Red Wine

150 ml (¼ pint) red wine
150 ml (¼ pint) water
1 cinnamon stick
50 g (2 oz) brown sugar
piece of orange or lemon peel
150 g (6 oz) pitted dates

150 g (6 oz) pitted apricots
150 g (6 oz) large pitted
  prunes
cream, yogurt or fromage
  frais

Prepare 1 or several days ahead: Put wine, water, cinnamon, sugar and peel into a saucepan, bring to the boil and simmer for 5 minutes. Add fruit and continue to simmer for 15 minutes, covered. Turn off and leave to cool and for the fruit to absorb the flavours.

To serve: Remove cinnamon stick and peel and turn the fruit and juices into a serving bowl. Serve the cream, yogurt or fromage frais separately.

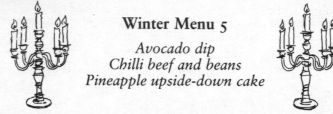

Winter Menu 5

Avocado dip
Chilli beef and beans
Pineapple upside-down cake

This meal has a South and a North American theme. It begins with a dip based on a Mexican sauce, guacamole, in which the bland flavour of avocados is spiced with lemon or lime, onion, tomato, garlic and green pepper. Make an hour or so ahead to allow the flavours to develop, remembering that avocado flesh blackens if exposed too long to the air. Eat the dip with tacos, tortillas or corn wafers and a selection of raw winter vegetables. Guacamole can be bought, but the tubs are small so you'll need more than one, and the flavour may need to be heightened with perhaps garlic or tabasco.

Chilli beef with beans, better known as *chili con carne*, does not come from Mexico as the name might suggest. It is a Texan idea of how a Mexican dish ought to be, rather in the same way as Raj curry bears only a passing resemblance to authentic Indian cooking. Nevertheless, although disowned by Mexico, this original Texan dish made with cubed meat is quite another thing to the hackneyed pub and wine-bar version made with mince. It combines spiciness with tomatoes and the bitter-sweetness of fresh coriander. Make it a day ahead if you like and reheat it on the day. Serve it either with plain rice and a bowl of watercress; or simpler still with plenty of garlic bread and a crisp green salad.

The meal ends with a famous North American cake which also can be eaten warm or hot, when strictly speaking it becomes a pudding. It's basically a Victoria sponge made in minutes in a blender or food processor, which when turned out is covered with a glistening topping of pineapple and melted brown sugar. Delicious just as it is, but even more so if sprinkled with spirit just before eating. You'll need a wide cake tin, about 25 cm (10 in) in diameter — a deep pizza pan is ideal — or if you have one, use a round cast-iron gratin dish. If you use a smaller tin, the cake will be deeper and take longer to cook: test by inserting a skewer, it should come out clean.

Avocado Dip

2 ripe avocados
grated peel and juice of 1 lime
   or lemon
1 small onion, finely chopped
1 clove garlic, chopped
1 dessertspoon tomato purée
2 dessertspoons finely
   chopped green pepper

several drops tabasco sauce
salt
selection of prepared raw
   vegetables, i.e. sprigs of
   cauliflower, sliced fennel,
   carrot, celery etc
1 packet tacos, tortillas or
   corn wafers

Prepare an hour or so aheaad: Cut the avocados in half, remove the stones and scoop out the flesh with a spoon into a bowl. Grate in the lime or lemon peel and squeeze in the juice. Mash well. Stir in the onion, garlic, tomato purée and green pepper. Add tabasco and salt to taste.

To serve: Put the bowl in the centre of a platter. Surround with vegetables and tacos, tortillas or corn wafers.

Chilli Beef and Beans

2 tablespoons oil
2 onions, chopped
750 g (1½ lb) lean stewing
   beef, cubed
2 cloves garlic, chopped
1–2 tablespoons chilli powder
½ teaspoon ground cumin
1 teaspoon dried oregano

2 tablespoons tomato purée
1 can Italian chopped
   tomatoes
salt
1 can red kidney beans,
   drained
handful fresh coriander,
   chopped

Prepare one day ahead: Heat the oil in a heavy-based flameproof casserole and fry the onions until golden. Add the meat and brown on all sides. Stir in the garlic, chilli powder and cumin and cook for a few minutes. Stir in the oregano, tomato purée and the canned tomatoes. Season with salt. Cover and simmer either on top of the stove or in the oven, Gas 3/325°F/160°C, for 1½–2 hours until the meat is tender. Add the drained beans and simmer a further 30 minutes. Eat right away, garnished with chopped coriander, or cool and set aside until the next day.

To reheat: Reheat on top of the stove or in the oven, Gas 4/350°F/ 180°C, for 30 minutes. Garnish with the chopped coriander.

Pineapple Upside-down Cake

for the topping:
50 g (2 oz) butter
50 g (2 oz) soft brown sugar
450 g (1 lb) can pineapple rings, drained

for the sponge:
100 g (4 oz) butter, softened
100 g (4 oz) caster sugar
2 eggs
100 g (4 oz) flour
1 teaspoon baking powder
kirsch, calvados or pear liqueur, optional

If eating cold, cook a day ahead: Heat the oven to Gas 4/350°F/ 180°C.

To make the topping: Slowly melt the butter and brown sugar in a 25 cm (10 in) tin or pan, turning it about to make sure bottom and sides are coated. Arrange the fruit over the base and slightly up the sides.

To make the sponge: Using a blender or food processor, blend butter and caster sugar until fluffy, then blend the eggs one at a time with the motor running. Turn off the machine, tip in the flour and baking powder and blend for a count of 5 until just mixed. Spread the sponge mix over the pineapple and bake for 35 minutes or until the top is golden brown and a skewer comes out clean. (Cooking time depends on the depth of your tin.) Allow to cool for a few minutes, then run a knife right round the edge and turn out on to a warm serving plate.

To serve: Serve hot, warm or cold sprinkled with spirit if using.

Winter Menu 6

Artichokes with peas
Cottage pie
Braised cabbage with juniper
Cranberry winter pudding

Artichokes, sweet-tasting peas, lettuce, bacon and lemon are a happy mix for the starter of this meal. Prepare it in a flameproof pan or dish that can be brought to the table. Never mind if it is a frying pan, the dish looks so pretty that only the most snobbish will object, and they have no place at a kitchen supper. Make sure when buying the canned artichokes that you get not the hearts but the saucer-shaped bottoms, which are a perfect receptacle for the filling.

For me, cottage pie spells childhood because it is what my brother and I always chose for our birthdays – that and Christmas pudding. It's a wonderfully comforting choice for a cold winter's evening and like all traditional dishes, there are dozens of different versions. This one with mushrooms and red wine is a little more sophisticated than the ones my grandmother and mother made. I hesitate to suggest serving tomato ketchup, but secretly I feel cottage pie is not the same without it. If you feel otherwise, offer instead a hot home-made sauce made with chopped onions and canned Italian chopped tomatoes, flavoured with garlic and herbs, or buy a commercial variety like *Sugocasa*. The pie can be assembled ahead of time and then baked before eating for about 45 minutes. However, if you opt for doing the whole thing just before supper, potatoes and filling will already be hot, so the pie will not need such a long time in the oven: it will only need about 20 minutes for the potatoes to brown. It's good with braised cabbage which in this recipe is a savoy, but you could use a red cabbage, in which case use red wine instead of white, cook it for half an hour longer and just before serving stir in a teaspoon of red wine vinegar and a tablespoon or two of redcurrant jelly. Or if you prefer just serve a simple green salad with a mustardy dressing.

Of course, you could follow my childhood example and end the meal with Christmas pudding; there are so many on sale up to Christmas that it would make an easy choice. I prefer to stop being nostalgic and go for something more refreshing, like cranberry winter pudding, which can be made 2 or 3 days ahead, and is in fact our old friend the Summer Pudding in disguise. It also uses frozen raspberries, which are widely available at this time of the year.

Artichokes with Peas

75 g (3 oz) concentrated
  butter
100 g (4 oz) streaky bacon,
  finely chopped
2 cans artichoke bottoms,
  drained and rinsed
1 can or jar *petits pois*

1 lettuce heart, shredded
1 teaspoon caster sugar
salt
freshly milled black pepper
juice of ½ lemon
handful chopped parsley

Can be prepared an hour or two ahead: Melt 50 g (2 oz) butter in a flameproof dish that can be brought to the table and fry the bacon for a few minutes. Remove from the heat and put in the artichoke bottoms, then fill each with a spoonful of *petits pois*. Sprinkle with the shredded lettuce and sugar. Season with salt and pepper and dot with the remaining butter.
To cook: Put over a high flame. When the pan is sizzling, cover with a lid or foil, lower heat and simmer until hot through, 15–20 minutes.
To serve: Sprinkle with lemon juice and parsley.

Cottage Pie

1 kg (2¼ lb) potatoes, peeled
2–3 tablespoons oil
2 onions, chopped
450 g (1 lb) extra lean minced
  beef

225 g (8 oz) mushrooms,
  sliced
2 cloves garlic, chopped or
  crushed
2 tablespoons tomato purée

150 ml (¼ pint) red wine
½ teaspoon dried oregano
salt
freshly milled black pepper

75 g (3 oz) butter
150 ml (¼ pint) milk
grated nutmeg

Can be prepared ahead: Put the potatoes into a pan of salted water, bring to the boil, cover and simmer until soft, about 20 minutes. Meanwhile, heat oil in a wide, heavy pan and fry the onions until soft. Add the meat and stir it until it is brown all over. Add the mushrooms and cook until they turn limp. Stir in garlic, tomato purée, the wine and oregano and season with salt and pepper. Simmer uncovered for 5–10 minutes. Drain the cooked potatoes and mash with 50 g (2 oz) of the butter and milk; season with salt, pepper and nutmeg. Put the meat sauce into a buttered pie dish, cover with the potato, smooth over the top and mark with the prongs of a fork.

To cook pie: Heat the oven to Gas 6/400°F/200°C. Dot the top with the remaining butter and bake for 40–45 minutes until top is golden brown.

Braised Cabbage with Juniper

2 tablespoons oil
150 ml (¼ pint) dry white
  wine
750 g (1½ lb) savoy cabbage,
  quartered, cored and
  shredded

3 tart eating apples,
  quartered, peeled and cored
1 teaspoon juniper berries
salt
freshly milled black pepper

To cook: Put all the ingredients into a heavy saucepan in the order given. Bring to the boil, cover, lower heat and simmer for 35–40 minutes. Just before serving, remove lid, raise heat and boil hard until almost all the liquid has evaporated.

Cranberry Winter Pudding

450 g (1 lb) frozen raspberries
225 g (8 oz) cranberries
100–150 g (4–6 oz) caster or
   vanilla sugar (see p. 186)
5 mm (¼ in) slices one-day-old

white bread, crusts
   removed
single cream, thick yogurt or
   fromage frais

Can be prepared up to three days ahead: Put the frozen raspberries in a colander over a bowl and leave to defrost for 2–3 hours. Pour the juice into a pan, add the cranberries and bring to the boil. Cover and simmer until the skins pop and the fruit softens, about 10 minutes. Add the raspberries, bring back to the boil, stir to mix and remove from heat. Add sufficient sugar to sweeten. Line a 1 litre (1¾ pint) pudding basin with slices of bread, plugging any gaps with small pieces. Pour in the fruit and juices, and make a lid with more bread. Cover with a saucer, weight it down with something heavy such as a flat-iron or tin and refrigerate.

To serve: Run a knife right round the edge and turn out on to a plate with a lip to catch the juices. Serve the cream, yogurt or fromage frais separately.

Winter Menu 7

Pâté with onion jam
Trout parcels
Bread and butter pudding

Onion jam, *confiture d'oignons*, comes from Provence and this recipe was charmed from the Auberge au Vieux Fusil in Issirac, where they serve it with their home-made pâté. I suggest you buy the pâté but find time to make the jam. It doesn't require much work, but needs to be cooked for 2½ hours. The onions, sugar and wine combine to make a golden brown preserve which is as good with other cold meats as it is with pâté. However, if making jam of any kind is not your concept of kitchen suppers, serve the pâté with gherkins, radishes and olives and a few rounds of very thinly sliced onion.

No, there's nothing new about trout parcels, but when the silver-wrapped fish are brought to the table, they never fail to add a festive air. All sorts of fish, including steaks or fillets, can be cooked in this way and the flavourings can be varied to suit your own herb garden and spice rack. Preparation can be done well ahead, the cooking needs no attention and everyone enjoys unwrapping their parcel to reveal the fish bathed in its own succulent sauce. Serve the trout with steamed small potatoes (see p. 80) such as Belle de Fontenay.

The newly fashionable old-fashioned bread and butter pudding offers comfort on a cold winter's night. It is lifted from the nursery class by the addition of brandy or calvados. It can be eaten hot, warm or cold, on its own or with cream or smetana, and will keep warm without spoiling in the turned-off oven. The secret is to prepare it at least half an hour ahead to allow the bread to soak up the milk and flavours of the dried fruit.

Pâté with Onion Jam

350 g (12 oz) bought coarse, country pâté
for the jam:
  900 g (2 lb) large onions, roughly chopped
  350 g (12 oz) soft brown sugar

65 ml (2½ fl oz) white wine
65 ml (2½ fl oz) red wine vinegar
juice of 1 lemon
1 jar gherkins
100 g (4 oz) unsalted butter
toast

Prepare one or several days ahead: Put the onions into a wide pan and add the sugar, wine, vinegar and lemon juice. Bring to the boil, stir well and simmer uncovered for 2½ hours, stirring from time to time. Raise the heat and boil until the liquid has reduced by half and the jam is a golden brown. Pour into a jar.

To serve: Serve the pâté, gherkins, onion jam and butter in separate bowls. Make the toast at the table. Store any left-over jam in a screw-top jar in the fridge.

Trout Parcels

olive oil
4 trout
4 sprigs of rosemary
2 teaspoons fennel seeds
4 dessertspoons crème fraîche
  (see p. 187)

4 slices lemon
50 g (2 oz) butter
salt
pepper
bunch of watercress

Can be prepared ahead of time: Cut 4 squares of foil each large
enough to enclose a fish, brush them with oil and lay a trout on
each. Put a sprig of rosemary, half a teaspoon fennel seeds and a
spoonful of crème fraîche into the cavity of each. Lay a slice of
lemon on top and dot with butter. Season with salt and pepper.
Fold into a loose parcel, twisting the ends. Put on a baking sheet,
slip it into a plastic bag and refrigerate until ready to cook.
To cook: Heat the oven to Gas 4/350°F/180°C and bake the fish
for 15–20 minutes.
To serve: Serve on a dish, surrounded by the watercress.

Bread and Butter Pudding

6 thin slices of white buttered
  bread, crusts removed
2 tablespoons raisins
2 tablespoons dried apricots,
  roughly chopped
2 eggs, plus 1 yolk

300 ml (½ pint) creamy milk
1 tablespoon brandy or
  calvados
2 or 3 tablespoons brown
  sugar
single cream or smetana

Prepare at least half an hour or several hours ahead: Butter an
oven-proof dish and lay the bread in it, sprinkling each layer with
dried fruit. Finish with a layer of bread. Beat the eggs in a bowl,
stir in milk and brandy. Pour over the bread and leave to soak
until ready to cook.
To cook: Heat the oven to Gas 4/350°F/180°C. Sprinkle the sugar
over the pudding and bake for 30–40 minutes.
To serve: Bring to the table and serve the single cream or smetana
separately.

Winter Menu 8

Potted prawns
Liver and onions
Marmalade apples

Potting fish in butter dates back a couple of centuries, and in our time it is an ideal way of using frozen prawns (making sure you allow plenty of time for them to defrost naturally before you begin). Not only is it a pretty starter, but the spices and lemon juice bring out the flavour of the shellfish. Do the potting a day or two ahead. All that needs to be done is to stir all the ingredients into melted butter and pour into individual pots. If you have a microwave, the butter can be melted in the pots themselves. Serve with hot toast which, if you have an electric toaster, can be made at the table.

Speed is the secret of cooking calf's or lamb's liver. It needs just enough time to seal the outside, leaving the inside pink and meltingly soft. Calf's liver is the best, but it is more expensive and in much shorter supply than lamb's. Whichever you buy, cut it into very thin slices or ask the butcher to do this for you. Before the others arrive, begin cooking the onions; they must be stewed with a very little sugar until they are soft and slightly caramelized. Don't cook the liver until the first course is over, as it takes less than 5 minutes. Serve with mashed potatoes which can be prepared before you sit down to eat, turned into an oven-proof dish, forked and dotted with butter and set in the oven to keep hot.

The dessert can be prepared an hour or two ahead to be popped into the oven as you begin the meal. It consists of halved, cored apples filled with marmalade which are baked in lemon juice and orange-flower water, or if you prefer use orange juice, or a fruit liqueur like calvados or Poire William. Around Christmas time, as an easy alternative to mince pies, you could fill the apples with mincemeat and douse them in brandy.

Potted Prawns

150 g (6 oz) Dutch or
   Normandy butter
½ teaspoon grated nutmeg
cayenne pepper
1 teaspoon ground ginger
freshly milled black pepper

salt
350 g (12 oz) prawns
4–8 lettuce leaves
1 lemon, quartered
8 slices toast

Can be prepared 1 to 2 days ahead: Melt butter in a saucepan, add the nutmeg, cayenne pepper, ginger, black pepper and salt. Divide the prawns between the pots. Pour in the butter and press the fish well down. Taste and adjust seasoning. Cool, cover and refrigerate. Remove from fridge an hour or so ahead.
To serve: Put lettuce leaves on 4 plates. Turn out the pots by first standing them for a minute or two in very hot water. Upturn them on to the lettuce. Garnish each plate with a lemon quarter and serve the toast separately.

Liver and Onions

3 or 4 tablespoons olive oil
900 g (2 lb) onions, peeled
   and finely sliced
1 teaspoon caster sugar
450 g (1 lb) calf's or lamb's
   liver, cut in thin slices

salt
pepper
juice of ½ lemon
2 cloves garlic, chopped
handful parsley, finely
   chopped

To cook the onions: Heat the oil in a large heavy frying pan (there should be enough to cover the base), add the sliced onions and the sugar and stir. Cover and leave to stew gently for 1 hour.
To cook the liver: Remove onions to a warm dish, cover with foil and keep in a warm place. Raise the heat, add a little more oil if necessary, and fry the liver quickly on all sides for 3–4 minutes. Season with salt and pepper, squeeze over the lemon juice and sprinkle with the garlic and parsley. Pile the liver on to the onions and serve.

Marmalade Apples

butter
4 large Coxs or other firm
  eating apples
4 dessertspoons Seville orange
  marmalade
juice of 1 lemon

2 tablespoons orange-flower
  water
4 tablespoons caster or vanilla
  sugar (see p. 106)
single cream, fromage frais or
  yogurt

Can be prepared an hour or two ahead: Butter a shallow oven-proof dish. Core the apples, cut them in half round the middle and lay them cut side down in the dish. Fill the cavities with marmalade. Squeeze over the lemon juice and pour over the orange-flower water. Sprinkle each apple with sugar.

To cook: Heat the oven to Gas 5/375°F/190°C and bake for 25 minutes.

To serve: Serve the single cream, fromage frais or yogurt separately.

Winter Menu 9

Black olives, oranges and fennel
Chicken with honey
Creamy rice pudding

This black olive, orange and fennel starter from Italy, *olive nere, arance e finocchi*, is both pretty and refreshing with its contrasting colours and flavours. Prepare it an hour or so ahead, longer if you prefer, to allow the oranges and fennel to soak up the flavours of the dressing. Buy the best black olives you can find, spiced or herbed ones from a delicatessen perhaps, or Greek *calamata*. Oranges are easy to peel provided you have a sharp knife, use a sawing motion and peel in a spiral, removing all the white pith with the skin.

  Buy farm-reared or corn-fed chicken for the main course, which was invented by my long-suffering husband, James, who loves to cook and too often finds me in the kitchen insisting on testing a new idea. It involves a number of stages, sautéeing, flaming and simmering and a last-minute addition of honey, but don't be put off, it's all quite easy and the result is delicious. Buy chicken portions or, if you want to save money and have time to spare, go for a whole chicken and joint it yourself. This doesn't take long, especially if you are equipped with a really good pair of kitchen shears. Serve the chicken with a spinach salad, dressed with a lemon-flavoured vinaigrette and throw in a handful of croûtons (see p. 183). Make sure there is plenty of Italian or French bread available. The same recipe could be made with rabbit portions.

A surprising number of people nurture a yen for the creamy rice puddings made by their mothers or grandmothers, which were so unlike the school dinner variety. A genuine rice pudding should emerge from the oven rich and thick, after hours of slow cooking. This pudding is delicious just as it is, although the truly nostalgic guest might well demand a bowlful of jam, and those who are unashamedly greedy or unruffled by health warnings might appreciate a dollop or two of double cream.

Black Olives, Oranges and Fennel

2 fennel bulbs, wiped and
  finely sliced
4–6 oranges
juice of ½ lemon
pinch of sugar
3–4 tablespoons hazelnut or
  olive oil

salt
freshly milled black pepper
225 g (8 oz) black olives
2 or 3 tablespoons chopped,
  roasted hazelnuts

Prepare at least an hour ahead: Arrange the sliced fennel in a shallow dish. Grate the peel of 2 oranges over it, taking care not to include any pith. Peel the other 2 oranges, then slice all 4 and lay on top of the fennel, discarding all pith and pips. Sprinkle with the lemon juice, sugar and oil and season with salt and pepper. Put the olives in the centre.

To serve: Sprinkle over the chopped hazelnuts and serve with the crusty bread.

Chicken and Honey

2 tablespoons olive oil
8 chicken pieces, skinned
25 g (1 oz) butter
1 onion, chopped
4 rashers streaky bacon,
   chopped
1 clove garlic, crushed

1 teaspoon soy sauce
2 tablespoons brandy or
   calvados
4 tablespoons dry white wine
salt
freshly milled black pepper
2 tablespoons honey

To cook: Heat the oil in a heavy flameproof casserole and fry the chicken until golden on all sides. Remove and keep warm. Wipe out the pan with kitchen paper and add the butter. When it sizzles, fry the onion and chopped bacon over a medium heat until just beginning to brown. Add the garlic and soy sauce and mix well. Return the chicken to the pan. Heat the brandy or calvados in a ladle or small saucepan, light it and pour it over the chicken. when flames die down, pour in the wine and season with salt and pepper. Cover and simmer for 45 minutes.

To serve: Remove the chicken to a warm serving dish. Place the pan over a high heat and reduce the sauce by half. Stir in the honey and pour the sauce over the chicken.

Creamy Rice Pudding

45 g (1½ oz) round Carolina
   rice
600 ml (1 pint) full-cream
   milk
25 g (1 oz) butter

2 tablespoons caster or vanilla
   sugar (see p. 186)
1 cinnamon stick or ½ teaspoon powdered cinnamon
jam or double cream

Prepare 3½ hours ahead: Heat the oven to Gas 1/275°F/140°C. Put all the ingredients except the jam and cream into a shallow, buttered baking dish and stir well. Bake for 3½ hours, stirring the pudding every hour.

To serve: Remove the cinnamon stick. Serve jam or cream separately.

Winter Menu 10

Mushrooms in vine leaves
Pigeons with bitter orange
Chocolate chestnut cream

The supper begins with an intriguing starter of dark mushrooms hidden between layers of vine leaves, that tastes as interesting as it looks. Vine leaves preserved in brine, imported from Greece, are quite widely available and can be found in many supermarkets, delicatessens or ethnic shops. The dish can be put together quite quickly just before it goes into the oven, or you can assemble it at any odd moment during the day. Serve these mushrooms with plenty of crusty bread.

The pigeon dish, *pigeons à la catalane*, comes from the most southerly corner of France, and is ideal for that moment when Seville oranges arrive from Spain, which is usually a week or so after Christmas. If you can't get hold of them, use instead half a sweet orange and an extra half lemon. Wood pigeons sold here are much tougher than the specially reared birds available in France, and need much longer cooking than the 45 minutes specified in the original recipe. I have adapted it with this in mind. Serve the pigeons with jacket or mashed potatoes and a can or two of little French peas, *petits pois*.

End the meal with an unashamedly rich and indulgent dessert bulging with chocolate, chestnuts, cream and a whiff of ginger. It's another of those sweets that chocolate mousse fans will adore without any of the fuss of beating and folding in egg whites. It can be made a day or two ahead.

Mushrooms in Vine Leaves

12–15 vine leaves
olive oil
450 g (1 lb) flat field
  mushrooms
1 teaspoon dried thyme
handful parsley, chopped

4 cloves garlic, chopped
50 g (2 oz) can anchovy
  fillets, chopped
freshly milled mixed or black
  pepper

Can be prepared ahead: Soak vine leaves for a few minutes in boiling water, drain and rinse. Lightly oil a shallow oven-proof dish and line it with half the leaves. Lay the mushrooms on top. Scatter over the thyme, parsley, garlic and chopped anchovy fillets and season with the pepper. Sprinkle with oil. Cover with the remaining leaves and a further sprinkling of oil.

To cook: Heat the oven to Gas 6/400°F/200°C and bake for 20–25 minutes.

To serve: Bring to the table and pull back and discard the top layer of vine leaves.

Pigeons with Bitter Orange

4 tablespoons olive oil
4 pigeons
150 g (6 oz) streaky bacon,
  chopped
12 whole, unpeeled cloves
  garlic
1 lemon, peeled and sliced
1 Seville orange, peeled and

sliced or ½ sweet orange
plus ½ lemon
150 ml (¼ pint) dry white
  wine
salt
freshly milled black pepper
handful chopped parsley

To cook: Heat the oil in a flameproof casserole and brown the pigeons all over. Remove and set aside. Add the chopped bacon and let it soften. Return pigeons to the casserole and add the garlic and sliced lemon and orange, discarding all pith and pips. Pour over the wine and season with salt and pepper. Cover and simmer gently for 2–2½ hours.

To serve: Serve from the casserole, garnished with the parsley.

Chocolate Chestnut Cream

150 g (6 oz) bitter chocolate
75 g (3 oz) butter
450 g (1 lb) can unsweetened
  chestnut purée
100 g (4 oz) caster or vanilla
  sugar (see p. 186)

2 tablespoons brandy
2 tablespoons chopped glacé
  ginger
150 ml (5 fl oz) double cream

Prepare several hours and up to two days ahead: Melt the chocolate with the butter, either in the microwave for a minute or two or in a low oven. Beat the chestnut purée with the sugar and brandy. When the mixture is creamy, beat in the melted chocolate and butter followed by the chopped ginger and the cream. Spoon into glasses or small pots and refrigerate.

Winter Menu 11

Little mussel pots
Hare with juniper and prunes
Baked mushrooms
Caramel custard

Prepare the starter, in which the mussels are heated in crème fraîche flavoured with garlic, parsley and parmesan, well ahead or put it together in minutes just before it goes into the oven. I suggest that to save time you use mussels canned in brine, quite definitely not ones in vinegar. It is of course delicious with fresh mussels but rather more trouble, as the mussels must be steamed open and then removed from their shells. Perhaps an excuse for treating yourself to a dish of mussels in cider (see p. 105) the night before and doing extra for this evening's supper. You would need about 450 g (1 lb) to fill the pots. Whichever you use, serve with lots of crusty bread.

Preparations for the hare begin 2–3 days ahead because, like all wild game, it benefits from being marinaded. This not only helps to tenderize the meat but also adds to the flavour. This recipe, *lièvre à la agenaise*, is spiced with juniper and sweetened with prunes which are a speciality of France's Agen region. The same variety are grown in California which is the source of most of the ones we buy. This dish is perhaps more sophisticated than the rabbit recipe in Autumn Menu 1, but it is just as easy to prepare. I suggest using hare portions, which can be bought in the super-market from early autumn until the end of February. A game dealer is likely to offer a whole hare, in which case ask him to joint it for you. Serve it with baked mushrooms and either jacket or mashed potatoes. It is one of those dishes which successfully reheats either on top of the stove or in the oven at Gas 4/350°F/ 180°C for 30 minutes.

The dessert, which should be prepared a day ahead, is a cross between burnt cream, *crème brulée*, and that restaurant favou-rite, *crème caramel*. It comes from the region which straddles the border separating south-western France and Spain, and is known variously as *crème catalane* and *crema catalana*. It is a simple custard made with eggs, milk and cornflour, traditionally served in wide, earthenware dishes, but what makes it special is that just before serving the custards are sprinkled with sugar and branded with a hot iron or salamander. The sugar caramelizes and forms a thin film over the top. Something of the same effect can be achieved by setting them under a hot grill.

Little Mussel Pots

1 can mussels in brine
freshly milled black pepper
4 cloves garlic, chopped or
  crushed
4 tablespoons chopped
  parsley

4 tablespoons crème fraîche
  (see p. 187)
2 tablespoons breadcrumbs
  (see p. 183)
4 teaspoons grated parmesan
sliced French bread

Can be prepared several hours ahead: Drain the mussels and divide them between 4 snail dishes or oven-proof ramekins. Season with pepper. Mix the garlic, parsley and crème fraîche and put a dollop on top of each pot, spread flat. Sprinkle over the breadcrumbs and grated parmesan. Cover and set aside in a cool place until ready to cook.

To cook: Heat the oven to Gas 6/400°F/200°C. Put the dishes on a baking tray and bake the mussels for 12–15 minutes until piping hot. Serve the bread separately.

Hare with Juniper and Prunes

4 hare portions, approx. 1 kg (2¼ lb)

for the marinade:
  300 ml (½ pint) red wine
  1 whole clove
  1 teaspoon allspice
  1 teaspoon juniper berries
  1 teaspoon peppercorns
  1 teaspoon dried thyme
  bay leaf
  1 garlic clove

12 large pitted Californian prunes
2–3 tablespoons armagnac or brandy
2 tablespoons flour
3 or 4 tablespoons olive oil
2 large onions, chopped
3 shallots, chopped
salt
freshly milled black pepper
1 teaspoon dried thyme
2 or 3 sprigs of rosemary

Two to three days ahead: Put the hare in a non-metallic bowl, pour over the wine and add all the other ingredients for the marinade. Leave to marinate for 2–3 days, turning the meat over once a day.

To cook: Soak the prunes in a bowl with the armagnac or brandy. Put the flour into a plastic bag, wipe the hare pieces with kitchen paper and add them, shaking well to coat them all over. Heat the oil in a flameproof casserole and brown the hare pieces, in 2 or 3 batches, removing them to a plate. Add the chopped onions and shallots and if necessary a little more oil, and cook until soft. Return the hare and strain over the marinade. Let it bubble, then add prunes and armagnac. Season with salt and pepper, sprinkle with thyme and put the rosemary sprigs on top. Cover and simmer for 1½–2 hours.

To serve: Remove rosemary sprigs before serving.

Baked Mushrooms

450 g (1 lb) flat mushrooms   1 teaspoon dried thyme
salt   50 g (2 oz) butter
pepper

Can be prepared several hours ahead: Butter an oven-proof dish and lay the mushrooms in it stalk-side up. Season with salt and pepper, sprinkle with thyme and dot with butter.
To cook: Heat the oven to Gas 6/400°F/200°C. Bake for 20 minutes.

Caramel Custard

600 ml (1 pint) creamy milk   1½ tablespoons cornflour
peel of 1 Seville orange or 1   7 tablespoons caster sugar
   lemon   4 egg yolks
1 cinnamon stick

Prepare a day ahead: Rinse out a saucepan with cold water, pour in the milk, add the peel and cinnamon, bring slowly to the boil and simmer for 10 minutes. Mix the cornflour with 3 tablespoons of sugar in a bowl and beat in the egg yolks one at a time until pale and frothy. Remove the peel and cinnamon from the milk and pour into the egg mixture. Return to the pan and stir over a medium heat until the custard thickens, about 5 minutes. At the first sign of a bubble, remove from heat, give a final stir and pour into 4 wide individual flameproof dishes, or one large dish. Set aside to cool. Refrigerate.
One to two hours before supper: Heat the grill. Sprinkle 1 tablespoon sugar evenly over each custard (or 4 over the large dish). Put under the grill until the sugar on the top melts and caramelizes. Set aside to cool.

Winter Menu 12

Chicory with croûtons
Breton fish casserole
The thirteen desserts

This final supper begins with a starter from Flanders in northern France. It uses golden heads of chicory tossed with croûtons and small pieces of bacon, flavoured with walnut oil and raspberry or wine vinegar.

The main course is based on the *cotriade* of Brittany, which is a cross between a soup and a stew, and rather like the southern French *bouillabaisse* it's really a glorified feast made with whatever the fishermen caught that day. Unlike *bouillabaisse*, it does not require any fish that is difficult to buy. The choice of fish is a matter of availability: I suggest monkfish, coley and rock salmon, with a smattering of mussels. But it could include any of the following fish and shellfish: conger eel, whiting, bream, plaice, mackerel, cod, haddock, wrasse, lemon sole, skate, hake, gurnard, garfish, lobster, crab and prawns. *Cotriade* is a complete meal needing no accompaniment other than garlic bread; or if there's no time to prepare this, simply toast sliced French bread, rubbed with garlic, at the top of the oven. Give everyone a soup spoon and a fork and a wide soup bowl. The soup is served in the cooking pot and the fish and vegetables on a platter. Everyone helps themselves to each. Cut the fish into chunks about 5 cm (2 in) square and cook the firmer fish (in this case monkfish) for a few minutes longer than the softer fish. In a perfect world you would use the skin, bones and heads of the fish to make the stock. This chore can be dispensed with by using water flavoured with concentrated Malaysian fish sauce, which is sold in bottles in Chinese and ethnic shops under such names as *Phú Quóc*, *Cá Sac* or *Nam Pla*. The mussels should be soaked for a few hours in cold, salted water, then washed and scrubbed. Any that are open and won't close when given a sharp tap should be thrown away.

The finalé comes from Provence. Traditionally served on Christmas Eve, but delicious at the end of any winter meal, the

thirteen desserts represent Christ and his apostles. They vary
from place to place but, especially for the busy cook, their great
attraction is they are all bought items based on seasonal fruits and
nuts and delicacies from the local baker. My list is not definitive.

Chicory with Croûtons

450 g (1 lb) golden-headed
  chicory, sliced
2 tablespoons walnut oil
100 g (4 oz) smoked streaky
  bacon, cut in small pieces
1 tablespoon raspberry or
  wine vinegar

salt
freshly milled black pepper
handful croûtons (see p. 183)
snipped chives or 1 clove
  garlic, chopped
handful parsley, chopped

To cook: Put the sliced chicory into a salad bowl. Heat the oil in a
frying pan and fry the bacon pieces until beginning to crisp. Tip
them over the chicory. Pour the vinegar into the pan, swill it
around and add to the salad. Add salt, pepper and croûtons and
mix gently. Sprinkle with the chives or garlic and the parsley and
serve.

Breton Fish Casserole

50 g (2 oz) butter
2 onions, chopped
2 leeks, sliced
2 cloves garlic, chopped
750 g (1½ lb) potatoes, peeled
  and cut in chunks
grated nutmeg
1–2 red chillies
1 teaspoon fennel seeds
2 or 3 sprigs of parsley
bay leaf
1 large can Italian chopped
  tomatoes

600 ml (1 pint) water
1 tablespoon Oriental fish
  sauce
cayenne pepper
500 g (1¼ lb) monkfish, cut in
  chunks
500 g (1¼ lb) mixture of rock
  fish and coley fillets, cut in
  chunks
500 g (1¼ lb) mussels, washed
salt
juice of ½ lemon
handful parsley, chopped

Can be prepared ahead: Melt the butter in a large, heavy flameproof casserole and fry the onions and leeks over a medium heat until they are soft, 5–10 minutes. Add the garlic, potatoes, grated nutmeg, chillies, fennel, sprigs of parsley and bay leaf. Mix and cook for a few minutes before adding the tomatoes, water and fish sauce. Season with cayenne pepper (add no salt at this stage). Cover and simmer until the potatoes are beginning to soften, 20–25 minutes. Either set aside to cool or finish the cooking.

To finish cooking: Bring the contents of the casserole back to the boil. Add the monkfish, cover and simmer for 3–4 minutes. Add rock fish, coley and mussels and simmer a further 5 minutes, until the mussels have opened. Add salt to taste if necessary.

To serve: Arrange fish, mussels and potatoes on a warm dish. Squeeze over the lemon juice and sprinkle with parsley. Serve the soup in the casserole.

The Thirteen Desserts

small clementines	hazelnuts
grapes	pears
dried figs	apples
lychees	honey cakes
box dates	oranges
walnuts	chocolate cinnamon hearts
almonds	

Prepare an hour or two ahead: Arrange everything attractively in bowls or on platters.

Dips and Bites

Banana raita
Cucumber raita
Chickpea and sesame dip
Bean dip
Blue cheese dip
Caper, olive and anchovy dip
Spicy pumpkin dip
Red pepper dip
Salted nuts and dried fruit

Olives in oil:
Greek green or black
French green
French black
Italian green or black
Spanish green
Spanish black

Dips and bites, either bought or home-made, are a quick answer to the problem of a starter. They can be eaten sitting around the table with a pre-supper drink. Below are some recipes but if there is really no time, the problem is solved by a quick visit to almost any supermarket to choose from their range of dips such as hoummus, taramasalata, tzatziki, feta and guacamole; these are all great standbys eaten with raw vegetables or a selection of the huge variety of bought bites now on sale alongside the ubiquitous potato crisp.

For example, you could offer ready-fried normal or miniature poppadums and masala puris with bowls of mango and lime chutney and one of finely sliced raw onions. These can be dipped into Greek tzatziki which has the same cooling effect as the cucumber and banana raitas given in this section.

Or serve tortillas, tacos, corn wafers or chips with hot Mexican chutneys and hoummus or guacamole, or make your own spicy bean, red pepper or pumpkin dip.

Or open a can of stuffed vine leaves, spear them with cocktail sticks and serve them with a bowl of thick Greek yogurt, or one of soured cream flavoured with chives.

Or serve a bowl of radishes to be dipped into salt and softened Dutch or Normandy butter.

Or dip sticks of celery in a quickly made *anchoïade* sauce: heat a little olive oil in a pan, add a can of drained chopped anchovy fillets, crush them to a purée, add a dash of vinegar and 150 ml ($\frac{1}{4}$ pint) of olive oil and bring to the table hot. Celery is delicious too with a cheese dip like feta, or the blue cheese dip given below.

Or serve taramasalata on slices of French bread toasted at the top of a hot oven, Gas 7/425°F/220°C, for 10 minutes, surrounded by lemon wedges.

Tapenade, the Provençal caper, olive and anchovy dip can be served in the same way, or is delicious as a dip for hard-boiled quail's eggs and a bowl of cherry tomatoes.

Or provide a loaf of Italian or French bread, a bowl of olive oil and others of olives and gherkins, a sharp knife and a whole spicy cured sausage like Spanish *chorizo* or Italian salami and let everybody carve their own.

Or perhaps have a quickly assembled selection of *crudités* arranged in small bowls on a tray or platter, choosing things like canned chickpeas, small quartered tomatoes and mushrooms, grated carrot, canned lentils, radishes and olives, all dressed with olive oil and flavoured with lemon juice, salt and pepper.

Or simply serve a selection of different olives, plain or spiced or salted fruits and nuts.

Banana Raita

This and the following cucumber raita are cooling Indian relishes or dips to be served with spicy bites like poppadums or Mexican corn wafers or tortillas.

2 bananas	2 cardamon pods
300 ml (½ pint) thick-set Greek yogurt	

Method: Mash bananas in a bowl, stir in the yogurt. Crush and split cardamon pods, remove seeds, pound and add to the bowl.

Cucumber Raita

2 tablespoons peeled and finely diced cucumber	1 tablespoon mint leaves, chopped
300 ml (½ pint) thick-set Greek yogurt	salt
2 spring onions, finely chopped	pepper
	paprika

Make at least 1 hour ahead of time: Put the diced cucumber in a strainer and leave to drain for at least 1 hour. In a small bowl mix yogurt, chopped spring onions, mint, salt, pepper and paprika. Stir in the cucumber just before serving.

Chickpea and Sesame Dip

The two following dips are quickly made using canned beans. This one is that most famous Middle Eastern dip *hoummus bi taheeni*, which is worth making if you've time, as it is cheaper and nicer than most commercial varieties. Tahini paste is found in health-food shops but if you have run out, add oil in its place.

1 can chickpeas, drained
2 cloves garlic, crushed
juice of 2 lemons
2–3 tablespoons tahini paste
salt
olive oil
paprika

Method: Put chickpeas, garlic, lemon juice and tahini paste into a blender. Blend until smooth. Season to taste with salt. Pile into a bowl. Just before serving dribble with olive oil and sprinkle with paprika.

Bean Dip

This spicy dip is adapted from an Egyptian recipe, *bissara*, which uses fresh broad beans. I find it works well using canned beans of all kinds.

1 can flageolet, haricot or
    kidney beans
3 cloves garlic, chopped
1 teaspoon tomato purée
salt
cayenne pepper
juice of ½ lemon
1 teaspoon ground cumin
handful chopped coriander,
    parsley and dill
2 tablespoons olive oil

Method: Put all the ingredients into a blender and process until smooth. Pile into a bowl and dribble over the oil.

Blue Cheese Dip

Make this dip with one of the subtle blue cheeses like Roquefort or Somerset blue-veined ewe's: nothing too harsh to catch the back of the throat. It is delicious with small ripe tomatoes, sprigs

of cauliflower, radishes and celery. It can also be made with
Greek *feta* cheese.

100 g (4 oz) blue cheese
3 or 4 tablespoons thick
  Greek yogurt
handful chopped dill, mint
  and parsley

squeeze of lemon juice
olive oil

Method: Mash the cheese and beat in the yogurt and herbs. Put
into a bowl, squeeze over the lemon and sprinkle with oil.

Caper, Olive and Anchovy Dip

This Provençal paste, *tapenade*, was probably brought to France
by the early Greeks. It can be eaten as a dip, spread on toast, used
to stuff hard-boiled eggs or as a base for a salad dressing. It can
also be spread on a chicken or leg of lamb before roasting.

225 g (8 oz) pitted black
  olives
1 clove garlic, chopped or
  crushed
50 g (2 oz) can anchovy
  fillets, drained
2 tablespoons capers

1 teaspoon Dijon mustard
freshly milled black pepper
pinch of dried thyme
nutmeg
1 teaspoon brandy or lemon
  juice
4 tablespoons olive oil

Method: Using a food processor, blend all the ingredients except
the oil. Add the oil drop by drop with the motor running, as for
making mayonnaise. Put into a bowl and serve at room temperature.

Spicy Pumpkin Dip

This North African dip *ajlouke de potiron* is quickly made using
canned pumpkin purée. It is a beautiful, bright orange, and has a
bitter-sweet, fiery taste.

1 can pumpkin purée
2 tablespoons olive oil
juice of 1 lemon
salt

2 cloves garlic, chopped
1 teaspoon *harissa* or hot
  chilli paste
1 teaspoon ground coriander

Method: Put all the ingredients into a food processor and blend.

Red Pepper Dip

This cardinal red dip is based on a North African recipe in which the papers are slowly roasted until the skins blacken and can be easily peeled away. Not difficult, but time-consuming. This version uses canned Spanish *pimientos*. It should be quite hot and spicy.

450 g (1 lb) can Spanish
  pimientos, drained
1 tablespoon tomato purée
1 teaspoon paprika

cayenne pepper
3 cloves garlic, chopped
1 teaspoon caraway seeds
1 tablespoon olive oil

Method: Put all the ingredients into a blender and blend until smooth.

Salted Nuts and Dried Fruit

At Christmas time, my grandmother always used to prepare little dishes of salted almonds and raisins, and this is a theme that can be adapted to all sorts of other nuts, seeds and dried fruits such as chopped apricots or figs, sunflower and pumpkin seeds, pine nuts, pecans and hazelnuts. Eaten while still warm they are extremely moreish.

2 tablespoons olive oil
100 g (4 oz) mixture of nuts
100 g (4 oz) mixture of dried
  fruits

salt
cayenne pepper
squeeze lemon juice
1 tablespoon chopped parsley

Method: Heat the olive oil in a small frying pan, add the nuts and fruit and fry quickly until the nuts begin to turn golden. Add the salt and cayenne pepper, squeeze over the lemon juice and sprinkle with the parsley. Drain on greaseproof paper before turning the nuts and fruit into a bowl.

Olives in Oil

Olives in various stages of ripeness from green through purple to black, often flavoured with spices and herbs, are sold all over the Mediterranean in shops and markets. They make most of the olives sold here seem insipid by comparison, but it's easy to flavour your own. Don't be put off by the large amount of olive oil involved: it can be used to give zip to salads when the olives are finished. Where dried herbs are specified use freeze-dried if you can; they are more expensive than ordinary dried but have more flavour. These olives will keep for months, provided you top them up with more oil as you use them and don't store them in the fridge – it is too humid and the olives can go mouldy.

Below are suggestions from Greece, France, Italy and Spain. The method is the same; only the flavourings are different.

Method: Put the olives into a 1 litre (1¾ pint) preserving jar and add all other ingredients, mixing well with a wooden spoon and covering completely with oil. Store in a cool, dry, dark place. Leave at least 1 week before eating.

Greek Green or Black Olives

350 g (12 oz) green or black
  olives
1 lemon, thinly sliced
1 tablespoon each dried
  thyme and oregano

2 whole cloves garlic
2 hot red chillies
approx. 450 ml (¾ pint) olive
  oil

French Green Olives

350 g (12 oz) green olives
3 bay leaves
2 or 3 sprigs of fresh or dried
   fennel, or 1 tablespoon
   dried fennel seeds
1 tablespoon coriander seeds

finely pared and chopped rind
   of 1 orange or dried orange
   peel can be used (see p.
   186)
olive oil

French Black Olives

350 g (12 oz) black olives
bay leaf
6 dried red chillies
2 tablespoons dried thyme

1 tablespoon fennel seeds
4 chopped cloves garlic
2 chopped shallots
olive oil

Italian Green or Black Olives

350 g (12 oz) green or black
   olives
3 or 4 cloves garlic, finely
   chopped

a handful of chopped basil
   leaves
olive oil

Spanish Green Olives

350 g (12 oz) large, green,
   unpitted olives, crushed
   lightly

6–8 cloves garlic, crushed
olive oil

Spanish Black Olives

350 g (12 oz) black olives
2 cloves garlic, crushed
2 tablespoons red wine
   vinegar

1 teaspoon of paprika
slice of lemon
olive oil

Three Aperitif Wines

Orange wine
Peach wine
Green walnut wine

If you have adventurous friends they will enjoy trying these aperitif or fortified wines from the South of France. The first two take just 2 weeks to prepare. The third, which is my favourite, takes rather longer and it depends on whether you know anyone with a walnut tree, because it is made in the summer when the walnuts are green and unripe and not usually sold in the shops. At first this may seem a difficulty, and it did to me. I couldn't think of anyone in this part of London who might help until I walked into the kitchen of a friend, Lynda Johnson, and there in a bowl on a table was a pile of green walnuts. So ask around and with luck you too will discover at least one tree in your neighbourhood. Of course, you could grow your own, but as it takes 12 years to produce its first crop, you might lose your enthusiasm to try the wine.

Orange Wine

This aperitif wine fortified with vodka is a simpler version of the Provençal *vin d'orange*. The oranges and spices are steeped in wine for a week before being sweetened and pepped up with the spirit. It is then ready to drink, but if well sealed will keep for some time. Serve chilled as it is, or freshened with a dash of soda water.

4 oranges, roughly chopped
½ lemon, roughly chopped
1 cinnamon stick
½ nutmeg
75 cl–1 litre (1¼–1¾ pints) dry white wine

100 g (4 oz) caster or vanilla sugar
150 ml (¼ pint) vodka, approx.

Prepare two weeks ahead: Divide oranges, lemon, cinnamon and nutmeg between 2 × 1 litre (1¾ pints) preserving jars. Cover with the wine. Seal and leave for 1 week.
Complete one week ahead: Put the sugar into a saucepan, strain

in the liquid from the jar and heat slowly, stirring from time to time, until the sugar has dissolved (don't let it boil). Allow to cool, pour through a funnel into bottles with screw caps, add vodka and top up with more wine if necessary. Seal with the caps and keep in a cool, dark place for at least 1 week before drinking.

Peach Wine

You can turn quite an ordinary white wine into a delicious aperitif using peaches. Peel them by steeping them for a few minutes in boiling water. Once the wine is made, drink it right away or cork it and keep in a cool place. The peaches themselves can be sliced and eaten on their own with cream or as part of a fruit salad.

3 ripe peaches, plus 3 extra peach stones	1 bottle dry white wine 100 g (4 oz) caster sugar
1 vanilla pod	150 ml ($\frac{1}{4}$ pint) vodka,
2 cloves	approx.

Prepare two weeks ahead: Put the whole, peeled peaches into a 1 litre ($1\frac{3}{4}$ pints) preserving jar with the vanilla pod and cloves and pour over the wine. Seal and leave for 1 week.

Complete one week ahead: Put the sugar into a saucepan, strain in the liquid from the jar and heat slowly, stirring from time to time, until the sugar has dissolved (don't let it boil). Allow to cool, pour through a funnel into a bottle with a screw cap and top up with vodka or brandy. Seal with the cap and keep in a cool, dark place for at least 1 week before drinking.

Green Walnut Wine

In midsummer, the green walnuts are just about ready to be picked and used to flavour this aperitif wine, *vin de noix* or as it is also known, *vin de la St-Jean*, midsummer day's wine. It is left to mature for 6–8 weeks, ready to be drunk on autumn evenings. The nuts must be picked before the shell has formed inside the outer skin. Test by piercing with a skewer: it should go right through. The juice of walnuts contains an indelible stain, so wear gloves when cutting them and use a heavy, sharp knife.

15 green walnuts, quartered
150 ml (¼ pint) vodka
225 g (8 oz) caster sugar
1 vanilla pod
1 cinnamon stick
2 litres (3½ pints) red or white wine, approx.

Method: Divide the ingredients between 2 × 1 litre (1¾ pints) preserving jars. Seal and leave for 6–8 weeks. Strain into clean bottles with screw caps. Seal with the caps and keep in a cool, dark place for at least 1 week before drinking.

Alcoholic Fruits

Old boy's marmalade
Fruit liqueurs
Prunes or apricots in Armagnac

Old Boy's Marmalade

It was a Swiss friend, Suzy Junor, who first served us *Rumtopf* or *confiture de vieux garçon*, as the French call it, although it bears no relation to marmalade, except that two of its main ingredients are fruit and sugar. The third is alcohol. Several years ago, she came back from Switzerland bearing one of the special stoneware jars. It was decorated in deep blue with cherries, peaches, plums and bunches of grapes, with the recipe in German on the back. All through that summer she collected each fruit as it came into maturity, and then one winter's evening after supper, served us ladlefuls in little glasses. We came away in something of an alcoholic haze.

Old boy's marmalade is the perfect answer to those hectic days when you long to offer something special but there's just no time. A jar made in the summer will provide a constant source of delicious desserts. A dollop will turn the most ordinary ice cream into a feast, or simply serve it in glasses or dishes, or more delicious still, spooned into the still warm coffee cups at the end of the meal.

Suzy followed the German recipe and used rum. The French use *eau-de-vie*, which is sold expressly for preserving fruits. I use vodka. You could use brandy or even gin. By mid-September put the jar in a cool, dark place and leave until Christmas. Don't worry if it ferments a little, this is normal. By Christmas, the fruits will have lost their individual colour and the liquid will be stained a deep red. When all the fruit is eaten, the remaining syrup can be used to add interest to ice cream or fresh fruit salads.

Ideally it should be made in a special *Rumtopf* or a large, glazed stoneware jar with a well-fitting lid. These can be expensive and difficult to find, so use instead a glass preserving or storage jar of at least 2 litres ($3\frac{1}{2}$ pints) capacity, because the fruit takes up a lot of room. Begin with 1 litre ($1\frac{3}{4}$ pints) of alcohol and only add more when the level of the fruit becomes higher than the liquid in the jar. Below is a selection of fruits you can use. It is not definitive and you can add more or less of any of them, but avoid citrus fruits. Make sure what you use is in good condition, clean and dry.

summer fruits as they come into season: cherries, strawberries (hulled) redcurrants, raspberries, apricots, plums and greengages (halved and stoned), peaches and nectarines (skinned, stoned and sliced), small ripe figs, seedless grapes

equal weight in granulated sugar

1–2 litres (1¾–3½ pints) vodka

Method: Pour 1 litre (1¾ pints) of vodka into the jar. Add the fruits as they become available, 225 g (8 oz) or so at a time. At the same time add an equal weight of sugar, sprinkling it over the fruit. Don't stir, but let the sugar weight the fruit down and submerge it. Top up with alcohol as necessary and keep the jar covered. It does not matter if there is not enough fruit to completely fill the jar, but make sure it is always submerged beneath the alcohol. At the end of summer, store the jar in a cool, dry place. Start eating the fruit around Christmas.

Fruit Liqueurs

Home-made fruit liqueurs are just as satisfying and far less trouble than all those jams and jellies which stacked the larders of every conscientious housewife in that never-never land of yester-year. They are wonderful to bring out at the end of a supper, giving a touch of how much you care, glittering like precious stones or the contents of those curvaceous jars which used to stand in every chemist's window.

There are 2 methods. The first for soft fruits, the second for firmer fruits. The fruit should be in its prime, clean and dry. On the Continent they sell clear, unflavoured spirit expressly made for preserving. Vodka is an excellent substitute, but you could use brandy, rum or gin.

Serve these liqueurs in small glasses or as the French do, after the coffee in the still warm cups.

Method 1

450 g (1 lb) of one of the following soft fruits: raspberries, strawberries, cherries, sloes, blackcurrants, mirabelle plums, grapes, blackberries

150 g (6 oz) caster sugar

600 ml (1 pint) approx. vodka

Prick cherries, sloes and mirabelle plums with a darning needle. Leave a tail of stalk on each cherry or grape. Fill a 1-litre (1¾ pints) preserving jar right to the top with the fruit. Pour in sufficient vodka to cover. Seal and leave in a cool, dark place for at least 2 months. Turn the jar over and over occasionally to make sure all the sugar dissolves.

To serve: Cherries and grapes can be served with the liqueur, to be picked up by their tails of stalk, but the others go mushy and the liqueur should be strained off into clean bottles. However, the fruit need not be wasted but can be puréed and folded into whipped cream, to make once-only fools and ice creams.

Method 2

450 g (1 lb) of one of the following firm fruits: apricots, plums, peaches, pears, figs, quinces

150 g (6 oz) caster sugar

150 ml (¼ pint) water

piece of orange peel

1 cinnamon stick or vanilla pod

600 ml (1 pint) approx. vodka

Quarter the fruit and crack the peach, apricot, nectarine and plum stones under a cloth with a hammer. Put fruit and stones into a 1 litre (1¾ pints) preserving jar. Put the sugar into a saucepan with the water, orange peel and cinnamon stick or vanilla pod and heat gently until the sugar is dissolved. Let this syrup cool and then pour over the fruit. Fill to the top with vodka and seal. Leave to mature in a cool, dark place for at least 2 months. Strain the liqueur into clean bottles. Eat the fruit with cream.

Prunes or Apricots in Armagnac

Both prunes and dried apricots preserved in alcohol make memorable desserts eaten simply with ice cream, fromage frais or cream. Armagnac is the traditional spirit for prunes but brandy, vodka or even gin can be used for either. Use French Agen or large Californian prunes (which are the same variety). The apricots should be the unsulphurated sort found in health-food or Asian shops, most of which come from Afghanistan and which I have praised elsewhere in this book.

450 g (1 lb) prunes or dried apricots

limeflower or ordinary tea or water

100 g (4 oz) sugar

1 vanilla pod or cinnamon stick

pared Seville orange or lemon peel

Armagnac

Method: Soak the prunes overnight in the freshly made tea, apricots in boiling water. Next day, drain the fruit and put into a 1 litre (1¾ pints) preserving jar. Add the sugar, vanilla or cinnamon and orange or lemon peel. Top up completely with spirit and seal. Leave to mature in a cool, dark place for at least 1 month. Turn the jar over and over occasionally to make sure the sugar dissolves.

To serve: Serve fruit and liqueur in small glasses.

Sundries

Breadcrumbs
Croûtons
Garlic breads
Mayonnaise
Vinaigrette
Preserved lemons
Dried peel
Vanilla sugar
Crème fraîche

Breadcrumbs

The breadcrumbs in the recipes are dried unless otherwise specified. Fresh breadcrumbs are quickly made with 2-day-old bread, crusts removed, in a food processor or by using a grater. There are several ways of preparing dried crumbs which can be stored for ages in a screw-top jar.

Method 1: Put fresh crumbs on a baking sheet and bake them in a warm oven until dry. Stir from time to time.

Method 2: Put fresh crumbs on a baking sheet, cover with kitchen paper and leave in a warm place until completely dry, about 1–2 days.

Method 3: Put pieces of stale French bread, crusts removed, on a baking sheet and leave in a warm oven until very dry. Put through a food processor or grate.

Croûtons

Croûtons, small bread squares fried or baked in oil, feature in many of the recipes. They can be bought ready-made in packets but they are not difficult to make and will keep for quite a time in a screw-top jar. Use day-old bread and cut into small cubes. Choose whichever method suits your temperament.

Method 1: Heat a frying pan, cover the base with oil and when it is hot add the cubes of bread and a crushed clove of garlic. Fry quickly for a minute or two until the bread is golden, turning the pieces over and over.

Method 2: Heat a frying pan, cover the base with oil and when it is hot add the cubes of bread and a crushed clove of garlic. Lower heat and fry as gently as possible for 30 minutes, turning the bread from time to time until it is golden and very crisp.

Method 3: Heat the oven to Gas 7/425°F/220°C. Pour some oil into a bowl, add the bread cubes and toss them briefly. Put them on an oiled baking sheet and bake until golden brown, turning them once or twice.

Garlic Breads

There is more than one way of making garlic bread and it doesn't have to be made with butter; olive oil is simpler and just as good. Below are 3 methods, the first two with olive oil and the third using butter.

Method 1: Heat the oven to Gas 7/425°F/220°C. Cut a long French loaf into slices and place them in a single layer on an oiled baking sheet. Sprinkle with 2–3 cloves of chopped garlic and plenty of olive oil. Bake for 5–10 minutes until golden brown.

Method 2: Heat the oven to Gas 7/425°F/220°C and toast slices of Italian or French bread until golden. Remove from the oven and rub them with the cut side of pieces of garlic. Put on to a warm plate, season with salt and pepper and sprinkle with olive oil.

Method 3: Heat the oven to Gas 7/425°F/220°C. Mash 100 g (4 oz) softened butter with 2 chopped cloves of garlic and a handful of parsley and season with a dash of lemon juice, salt and pepper. Slice the loaf lengthwise and spread one side with the garlic butter. Sandwich the 2 halves together and cut into portions, laying them down the length of a piece of kitchen foil. Wrap into a parcel and bake for 10 minutes.

Mayonnaise

Maybe you have your own foolproof method of making mayonnaise, if so please tell me. If you have a food processor you will have a recipe in the booklet provided and if it works, use it. I have tried all sorts of promised miracle methods but none seem as good as the mayonnaise beaten by hand. It doesn't really take long but it does need faith. As soon as you begin to doubt it will work, it separates. At least, that's how it seems. Follow the golden rule: everything, bowl, oil and eggs, must be at room temperature. Choose a low work surface, make it in a wide bowl with a cloth underneath it to prevent it slipping, and beat with a wooden spoon. Beat always in the same direction. Thoroughly mix the yolks, mustard, salt and pepper before beginning to add the oil, drop by drop. Keep beating as you add the oil, and as the mayonnaise thickens increase the flow but without ever being reckless. Once it is thick, add lemon juice or vinegar to give it bite and to thin it a little. Always use a good quality oil, all olive if you like, but if this seems too strong use some sunflower oil as well. If the mayonnaise separates, start again with a fresh egg yolk, gradually beating in the curdled mixture.

2 egg yolks	300 ml ($\frac{1}{2}$ pint) oil
1 teaspoon dry mustard	1 or 2 teaspoons lemon juice
salt	or vinegar, to taste
freshly milled black pepper	

Method: Break the yolks into a wide bowl. Add mustard, salt and pepper and thoroughly mix using a wooden spoon. Gradually beat in the oil, drop by drop, increasing the flow as the mayonnaise thickens. Finally add lemon or vinegar to taste.

Vinaigrette

Vinaigrette is quickly made using a screw-top jar. I find it is handy too to make more than I need, and for this I use an empty oil or vinegar bottle. I use a funnel and start with a teaspoon or two of mustard, salt and pepper and then add vinegar to about one-sixth of the bottle which I then fill to about 5 cm (2 in) below the top with olive oil. Finally I add a whole peeled clove of garlic. It must be well shaken each time it is used.

Preserved Lemons

The peel of lemons preserved in salt and lemon juice features in many North African dishes. It adds a subtle but distinct flavour, without the bitterness associated with fresh lemons. You can buy preserved lemons in upmarket food outlets, but they are easy to prepare and will keep for a year provided you top them up with more salt and lemon juice as you work through the jar. The lemons must be kept for a month before using. Only the peel is used, the lemons themselves must be thoroughly rinsed and the flesh discarded. Should a mould form in the jar, don't worry,

simply rinse it away. To fill a 500 ml (18 fl oz) preserving jar, you
will need:

4–5 whole ripe lemons   100 g (4 oz) salt
juice of 2–3 lemons

Method: Quarter each lemon vertically almost to its base – it
must not fall apart. Hold it over the jar, open it out and sprinkle
the flesh liberally with salt. Reform and put into the jar, packing
them tightly and pressing them down to release their juice.
Sprinkle over any remaining salt and squeeze over sufficient
freshly squeezed lemon juice to completely cover. Seal the jar and
store in a dry, warm place for a month, turning it over every day.

Dried Peel

It's very easy to dry the peel of citrus fruits and a supply is a useful
store standby when you haven't a fresh orange or lemon handy.
Simply remove the peel from the fruit in a spiral, using a swivel-
bladed peeler, and hang it to dry in a warm place. Once hard,
store in a screw-top jar. One or two pieces buried in caster sugar
will perfume it beautifully.

Vanilla Sugar

Vanilla pods come from an orchid found in the tropical rain
forests. They seem expensive when compared to vanilla essence,
but when you consider that a vanilla pod can be used again and
again (simply rinse and dry it and bury it in a jar of sugar), it soon
becomes apparent that they are not expensive at all. The sugar
itself takes on the vanilla's subtle aroma and can be used in any
recipe which calls for both. As you use the sugar, keep topping up
the jar and only replace the vanilla pods when they cease to be
effective.

Crème Fraîche

Crème fraîche is French soured cream with a much higher fat content than the kind we produce. It keeps well and is ideal in cooking as it does not curdle if boiled and adds a distinctive nutty flavour. It is widely available but if you cannot get it, it is simple to make your own. Stir a carton of ordinary soured cream into twice its volume of double cream and leave for several hours in a warm place before refrigerating.

Concentrated and Clarified Butter

Butter when used for frying tends to burn quite easily and leaves a residue of black flecks in the food. This can be overcome by using concentrated butter, sold in many supermarkets among the cooking fats. Originally concentrated butter was adopted as a means of reducing the Common Market butter mountain; this was achieved by subjecting it to a clarifying process which removed the water content and decreased its bulk. Clarifying butter also removes the salty particles which burn and blacken when ordinary butter is heated, so when it was decided to sell off some of the mountain, cooks quickly realized its advantages over ordinary butter for frying. Not only is it cheaper but it saves the time-consuming process of clarifying butter in the kitchen.

If you can't get concentrated butter use ordinary butter instead, adding a little oil which will help to prevent it burning. Or if you've time, make a supply of clarified butter yourself by heating 225 g (8 oz) butter gently, let it bubble until a scum forms on the top and then strain it through a sieve lined with damp muslin into a warm jar. Keep refrigerated.

Index

The entries for actual recipes are in bold type. Lighter type is used for ideas for dishes, names of people, etc. The names of foreign dishes mentioned in the text are in italics.

Also by Jenny Baker

Simple French Cuisine

This book is a feast of practical and delicious meals which are not only simple to prepare but give impressive and authentic results. It's also a fascinating guidebook – an ideal companion for French holidays as well as English kitchens.

'This is a remarkable book, evocative, down-to-earth, firmly rooted in the Languedoc, where people have done themselves proud for centuries.' *Daily Telegraph*

'It is also delightfully written – as much at home on the bedside table as in the kitchen – and filled with delicious reliable recipes.' *Sunday Telegraph*

The Student's Cookbook

Are you living away from home for the first time and fed up with take-aways? Would you like to cook for yourself but don't know how to begin?

'An absolutely excellent exposition of what food to buy and how to cook it when you're young, hard up and new to the art.' *She*

'A delightful, unpretentious book which can be wholeheartedly recommended.' *Cambridge Student Magazine*

Vegetarian Student

'The recipes are imaginative and the preparation and cooking methods realistic.' *Over 21*

'An excellently practical and informative book.' *New Statesman*

'Full of advice on how to make healthy, tasty vegetarian meals on a small budget.' *The Scotsman*